Understanding Your One-Year-Old

Understanding Your Child Series

The Tavistock Clinic has an international reputation as a centre of excellence for training, clinical mental health work, research and scholarship. Written by professionals working in the Child and Family and the Adolescent Departments, the guides in this series present balanced and sensitive advice that will help adults to become, or to feel that they are, "good enough" parents. Each book concentrates on a key transition in a child's life from birth to adolescence, looking especially at how parents' emotions and experiences interact with those of their children. The titles in the Understanding Your Child series are essential reading for new and experienced parents, relatives, friends and carers, as well as for the multi-agency professionals who are working to support children and their families.

other titles in the series

Understanding Your Baby
Sophie Boswell
ISBN 1 84310 242 0

Understanding Your Two-Year-Old
Lisa Miller
ISBN 1 84310 288 9

Understanding Your Three-Year-Old
Louise Emanuel
ISBN 1 84310 243 9

Understanding Your One-Year-Old

Sarah Gustavus Jones

Jessica Kingsley Publishers
London and Philadelphia

First published in the United Kingdom in 2004
by Jessica Kingsley Publishers
116 Pentonville Road
London N1 9JB, England
and
400 Market Street, Suite 400
Philadelphia, PA 19106, USA

www.jkp.com

Copyright © The Tavistock Clinic 2004

Library of Congress Cataloging in Publication Data
A CIP catalog record for this book is available from the Library of Congress

British Library Cataloguing in Publication Data
A CIP catalogue record for this book is available from the British Library

ISBN 1 84310 241 2

Printed and Bound in Great Britain by
Athenaeum Press, Gateshead, Tyne and Wear

For Rebecca and Matthew

Acknowledgements

With grateful thanks to the many parents and friends who have generously shared their thoughts and experiences with me. Above all, to the young children whose stories have made the writing of this book possible.

Contents

Foreword

The Tavistock Clinic has an international reputation as a centre of excellence for training, clinical mental health work, research and scholarship. Established in 1920, its history is one of groundbreaking work. The original aim of the Clinic was to offer treatment which could be used as the basis of research into the social prevention and treatment of mental health problems, and to teach these emerging skills to other professionals. Later work turned towards the treatment of trauma, the understanding of conscious and unconscious processes in groups, as well as important and influential work in developmental psychology. Work in perinatal bereavement led to a new understanding within the medical profession of the experience of stillbirth, and of the development of new forms of support for mourning parents and families. The development in the 1950s and 1960s of a systemic model of psychotherapy, focusing on the interaction between children and parents and within families, has grown into the substantial body of theoretical knowledge and therapeutic techniques used in the Tavistock's training and research in family therapy.

The *Understanding Your Child* series has an important place in the history of the Tavistock Clinic. It has been issued in a completely new form three times: in the 1960s, the 1990s, and now, in 2004. Each time the authors, drawing on their clinical background and specialist training, have set out to reflect on the extraordinary story of "ordinary development" as it was observed and experienced at the time. Society changes, of course, and so has this series, as it attempts to make sense of everyday accounts of the ways in which a developing child interacts with his or her parents, carers and the wider world. But within this changing scene there has been something constant, and it is best described as a continuing enthusiasm for a view of development which recognizes the importance of the strong feelings and emotions experienced at each stage of development.

The conclusion of the first volume commented on the changes in the first year of life, from being a baby towards being a toddler. However, the story so far would suggest that movement towards another place in development terms is a complex process. The aspiring toddler of today is accompanied by the experience of being the baby of not-so-long-ago, and this can be difficult, both for the one-year-old and for parents. Who and what do you talk to in such circumstances: the raw appearance of vulnerability and of panicky states of mind, or the sure steps towards more competence, confidence and better communication? In a moving account, Sarah Gustavus Jones considers how to respond to both, and how one is helped in this task by being in touch with a view of development that can tolerate and make sense of the sudden intrusion of seemingly past events and "old" feelings.

Jonathan Bradley
Child Psychotherapist
General Editor of the Understanding Your Child series

Introduction

So the first year is over. Your baby has already come through an incredible journey, emerging as a newborn and, day by day, being raised up to the relative sturdiness of a one-year-old. Looking back, it's not always easy to see how it happened.

One mother talked about her baby Simon's first year as a kind of dream-like blur – floods of activity and intense feelings interspersed with some blissful moments of quiet and deep joy, and hardly ever enough sleep. Sometimes it can feel like the new baby's needs dominate everything else and everybody else, and parents can feel desperate for some time to themselves. The intensity of the mother–baby relationship, so all-consuming at first, is essential for the physical and emotional survival of tiny newborns. They need to be held, fed, cleaned and comforted almost constantly. When they are sleeping, those around them often simultaneously collapse with exhaustion. It can be the hardest job in the world but can also be the most rewarding, although the emotional cost of this job invariably exceeds all expectations.

At the age of one year, babies are still very physically and emotionally dependent on others, but the challenges and demands have changed. The intense, full-on, seemingly every-second-of-the-day care may no longer be needed (at least not all the time). But struggling to understand your baby and respond to him or her in a way that helps, remains the fascinating and endlessly challenging preoccupation that faces parents and carers of one-year-olds. All this happens against the backdrop of an emotional process that begins at birth, and continues for a lifetime, as your baby grows towards being a separate, secure and independent person.

At Simon's first birthday, his mother said she was only just beginning to wake up to feeling more like herself again, rather than simply "Simon's mother". Much as she loved Simon and enjoyed her new role, it was good to have some glimmers of perspective back in her life. As his mother talked, Simon sat on the floor close to her, engrossed by the activity and faces around him at his small birthday party. It seemed that he also was beginning to take a more independent interest in things outside the intensity of his relationship with his mother. From his point of view, and his position of security next to her, the world seemed more and more fascinating.

So how does the world look to a one-year-old? And when a baby does not have the words to explain things to us, how can we begin to try to understand? T.S. Eliot faced this challenge when he imagined himself into the mind of a baby in *Animula* (1929). In this poem Eliot described a baby growing into a very small child and discovering things that fill him with wonder and surprise.

Occasionally we come across something that encapsulates our own experience in a way that can stop us in our tracks with its accuracy. We could be reading a book, listening to the radio or to a piece of music, watching a play or film, visiting a gallery, or simply having a close conversation. Then suddenly, someone else's experience, wisdom or imagination captures the essence of what is true for us. We are given our own experience back through someone else's expression, and we know it more fully as a result. The feeling of this is so deeply satisfying that it's almost beyond words. It's as if being understood grounds us more fundamentally to our own personality and helps us to be more ourselves, giving a greater depth to our character.

Perhaps this is why parents continue to struggle to understand their babies at the same time as attending to their physical needs. It seems to involve being interested in getting to know their real babies, in the hope of developing their personality as far as it can go, or raising them up to reach their full potential. It's not idealized or sentimental but it is motivated by love and involves engaging with the baby's experience in a genuine sense – the good and the bad. In this way it's linked to a recognition of what is true and real in the life and personality of babies, understanding them and, over time, helping them to know themselves and become more themselves. Parents and carers are the potential artists in their baby's world, and the creativity involved in trying to understand them, and sometimes succeeding, can be as enriching and fulfilling for the adult as it is for the child.

1

Brave New World

How do conversations start?

When asked at what stage she started talking to her baby daughter Ayesha, the mother thought for a moment and then replied that it was before she was born. Apparently Ayesha would make a series of very distinct, quick movements inside her and her mother would stroke her stomach and ask what she was up to. At this Ayesha would quieten and seem "to listen" to her mother's voice as she continued talking to her. When her mother stopped talking and stroking, the quick movements started up again, and they ceased when her mother resumed talking and stroking. This kind of reciprocal "conversation" became something of an evening routine between them through the last months of pregnancy.

Ayesha's mother then recalled that when she went into hospital for the birth, after a promising start suddenly everything went quiet. With things progressing so slowly, the midwife suggested that Ayesha's mother talked to the baby and tried to encourage her to come out – it was a great world outside and she needn't be scared; she could breathe fresh air and grow bigger. So the conversation between Ayesha and her mother resumed and eventually the labour moved on.

This story may sound quite bizarre, but it's also a surprisingly familiar one to many parents. Mothers in particular often instinctively start the "conversation". Thinking about it in this context, what does the development of words and language mean to your one-year-old?

In Ayesha's case, the "conversation" started as her mother responded to her daughter's quick movements by stroking her stomach. At the same time questions like "What are you up to?" seemed to show her thinking about

Ayesha, trying to understand her mood and calm her as a response. Ayesha's communication was received and contained by her mother's understanding, wrapped in her words and comforted by her stroking. Each one seemed to take turns in communicating and then wait and listen while it was the other's turn. This turn-taking was initiated by Ayesha's mother, as if she was showing her unborn baby how a conversation between them could work. The rhythm of listening, trying to understand and then responding seemed to be more important than the words themselves at this stage.

Something similar was described by Louise's mother. When Louise was three months old she was looked after for a couple of hours a week by Nina, a Spanish babysitter, giving Louise's mother a break. Nina told Louise's mother that when Louise seemed fretful and missing her, she found herself talking to her in Spanish. Although Nina's English was excellent, speaking to the baby in her mother tongue felt more natural and spontaneous, and it seemed to calm and please Louise.

At this early stage, the empathetic warmth and tone of a conversation communicates itself more than specific words, in terms of thoughtful attention to the baby. It seems more to do with the adult's state of mind – open to holding the baby's experience, whatever that experience may be. A parent or carer in touch with their own internal, natural resources – possibly linked to their mother tongue – can hold the baby's experience in such conversations, as Nina seemed to do so helpfully for Louise. It's also interesting that as the months passed, Nina felt she wanted to speak in English more, as if the words themselves were becoming increasingly significant to Louise as she approached her first birthday.

In a similar way, many parents and carers are convinced of the value of talking to their pre-verbal babies. They can recount long, friendly conversations about the relative price of nappies, or possible techniques for unblocking the kitchen sink, during which the baby will interject with squeaks, gurgles and smiles at significant places. They will swear that their babies positively like being included in this way, long before they can talk in words. The added bonus is that it somehow keeps the baby happy while allowing wonderfully useful periods of time for multitasking. Of course, your one-year-old will let you know when the conversation has become boring. Words are not necessary for this either.

But as well as learning about basic rules governing the art of conversation – the rhythm of taking turns and getting used to a whole range of vocabulary – the most significant thing for babies in such conversations is the feeling of an emotionally containing presence. Whereas for a tiny baby there may be no substitute for being held in mother's arms when comfort is needed, many one-year-olds can now be emotionally held by words and sentences for significant periods of time. This kind of psychological holding with words and the sound of a friendly, communicative voice is very important and has far-reaching implications. Your baby will be recognizing something about the way words can contain and hold an experience together, just as they feel they are being emotionally held together by the current "conversation". Even if they don't yet understand what all the words mean, they will be getting the message that words have meaning and that words can relate to an experience of being emotionally held and contained in someone else's mind.

First words

Eventually the time will come when the first words are spoken. Some babies will speak earlier and others later, but generally the time is somewhere towards the end of the first year. The build up is usually highlighted by a period of experimental "babbling" where a series of sounds are linked together and seem to be played with and enjoyed by your baby: "B-b-b-b-b-b-b-b-b-b-b", "D-d-d-d-d-d-d-d-d-d-d", "M-m-m-m-m-m-m-m-m-m-m-m". These are often the first sounds and can quite quickly turn into Mama and Dada.

Beatrice's mother talked about her saying her first, very distinct words, apart from Mama and Dada. They were "bird" and "good girl" and she spoke them around her first birthday. "Bird" was an important word for both of them as they had previously spent a lot of time during Beatrice's first summer on a rug in the garden, watching the birds and having long "conversations" about them. So her mother was delighted and looked forward to new words every day. In fact, what happened was quite the opposite. Beatrice went back to babbling for the next couple of months. Although language seemed to be there for her, the timing may not have felt right to move forward with it at that stage. When she did say "bird" again it was to her grandmother, with her mother standing close by. She was now about 14 months and this time "bird" came alongside a rush of other new words – "cow" and "lunch". It felt as though she had been storing up a complete vocabulary in her mind, available for when she felt ready to use it.

Every new move forward for your one-year-old comes at a cost. The world of language is a joy and can link you up with others in a wonderful, enriching way. At the same time, making new links with others necessarily means being more separate from the intensity of that first mother–baby relationship. This is an emotional leap as well as a cognitive one and babies need to do it in their own time. For Beatrice words seemed to represent her growing capacity to be more securely separate from her mother and to start a conversation with someone else. She appeared to be cognitively ready to use words earlier than she was emotionally ready.

So when the first words come they may be particularly tentative for some babies. This is the stage when parents and carers often take extra time to listen carefully to their baby, wondering with them what they may be trying to say, gently encouraging them and building up their confidence. Sometimes they may put particular meaning to their baby's communications, trying to understand their thoughts and giving them simple sentences that can hold the thoughts together.

A conversation between Jordan and his auntie went something like this. Jordan began smiling, laughing and pointing under his high chair. His auntie, who was supervising tea, asked what he was looking at. "Ball," he said, with some effort, getting his mouth around the new word. "Oh! You said 'ball'," she replied, delighted. "Yes, that's your red ball." They looked at the ball together quietly for a while. Then she asked, "Do you like your ball?" Jordan beamed at her and quietly said "Ball" again. "You like your ball," she said. Tea continued, with various comments about the ball from both sides. Jordan seemed to be enjoying the conversation very much and became increasingly confident and voluble about the ball. Finally he seemed to reach a climax, wildly waving his arms and shouting "Ball! Ball! Ball!" At this point his auntie asked, "Are you wanting to hold your red ball? You really do like that ball! Shall I get the ball for you?"

This kind of helpful encouragement and attention is usually more possible with first-born children, who can benefit from the luxury of their parent or carer having more time for one-to-one conversations – it certainly helped Jordan's confidence. In busier times, or with more children around, babies often observe more and talk later.

Lucy's mother joked about the very first words of her baby daughter, which she felt rather aptly captured the strong personality of her one-year-old. In fact she recalled two words that seemed to come together: "Me!" and "No!" Lucy said an adamant "No!" to being put in her high chair. In the same way, she said "No!" to her shoes being put on for her, insisting it should be "Me!" The power of language cannot be underestimated. Being able to say "No" to something or someone is very empowering. It can transform your baby's world.

The world of language and imagination

Songs and nursery rhymes use language in a way that really appeals to one-year-olds. At around the time Neha was just starting to talk, her father would often sing her Nelly the Elephant during her evening bath time. They developed a little routine together:

Father: Nellie the elephant packed her...

Neha: Tunk!

Father: ...and said goodbye to the circus. Off she went with a trumpety trump...

Neha: Tunk! Tunk! Tunk!

Books of nursery rhymes can also be read together over and over again at this age; babies love the repetition. It seems to be a satisfying way of starting to have control over language – you know what is coming next and you can begin to fill in the gaps. There is also a musical quality to the language of rhyme – like songs – that seems to make it particularly appealing, and the story contained within the rhyme is short, simple and highly imaginative. There are many well-illustrated nursery rhyme books available in good book-shops and libraries. Sometimes the paperback versions are more manageable for small hands and allow more enthusiastic book-loving babies to begin to look at the pictures independently too. But initially there is no substitute for taking the time to sit together with a book of nursery rhymes, reading the words and having a conversation about the pictures.

Also popular at this early stage are the books that simply consist of pictures and one-word descriptions. Although they don't look particularly inspiring on the shelf, babies just learning to talk seem to love these books, perhaps enjoying being able to understand their more simple format and master them relatively quickly. Pointing to the word, relating it to the picture and then talking about the picture in more detail brings immense satisfaction and soon your one-year-old will be "reading" the book to you. The sense of achievement at this again builds up confidence and helps your baby to recognize words and language as something increasingly within grasp. Tapes and

CDs of songs and nursery rhymes are also good value and all encourage a strong language base.

Gradually your baby will become interested in books with stories, but keep them simple at first and, as with everything else, respect your instinct and go at your own baby's pace.

Jack's mother talked about feeling disappointed that he would never sit on her lap long enough to read a book together. Whenever she tried he just slammed the book shut with his hands and struggled to get down. Eventually she decided not to push it any further and tried to accept that he just wasn't interested in books. However, when it no longer seemed to be a difficult issue between them, Jack miraculously became more interested in books of his own accord. But he liked to choose his own stories.

When they are ready to cope with stories, very young children are fascinating in the way they latch on to particular storybooks. They are often not the books we would expect them to like, but they will be asked for again and again. It seems to be something in the story that unconsciously engages them in some way, and they can explore their feelings through the story while still keeping those feelings (which may be experienced as overwhelming) at a safe distance.

Rachel's mother said that Rachel had always enjoyed being read to and there was one book she loved. It was John Burningham's *Avocado Baby* (1994) and was all about a baby who didn't eat much until one day her mother, by now upset because the baby wasn't growing big and strong, discovered an avocado pear in the fruit bowl. She mashed it up and gave it to the baby. The baby loved it and grew superhumanly strong on the diet of avocados – breaking out from the straps on the high chair, pushing cars, carrying shopping, chasing burglars and generally rescuing the family from disaster. At 18 months Rachel seemed to find this book very satisfying and awe inspiring, returning to it again and again.

Through stories, songs and nursery rhymes, parents and carers are introducing their babies to the creativity of language and narrative. They are reinforcing an understanding of the way language can be used to hold a story together – their story or perhaps someone else's. Just as your baby relies on your words and understanding to give meaning to his or her experience, so some stories from books can be recognized as holding experience together in a similar way. Later they will also gradually recognize how they too have access to making up their own stories – through language and imagination – and how they can work through their own feelings in this process as well as imagining themselves into someone else's shoes. As budding authors of their own narratives they can begin to extend their stories even further through the development of imaginative play.

First steps

Peter was just three years old when his baby sister, Christine, was born. He seemed to accept the new situation without much fuss and as she grew older he rather liked the way Christine would follow him around the room with adoring eyes, clearly finding him the most fascinating individual. They even began to enjoy playtimes in the same room. Their mother would often put a clean, soft rug on the floor for Christine to lie on, with a collection of her own special baby toys around her. Peter would be in the same room with his toys, very much in charge of the game. Then one day, everything changed. Their mother described Peter's voice of horror at what he witnessed when he called her loudly and urgently into the room: "Mummy! She's mooooooooving!"

Everything does change when your baby starts moving. In the same way that babies talk at different times, so they take their first steps at different times, although they have usually started to crawl in some kind of fashion by the time they are around a year old.

Susan began to crawl a few days before her first birthday. When a visitor called at the flat later that week, her father was keen for his daughter to demonstrate. He put Susan on the floor, calling her towards him, arms outstretched. She turned and looked at him and contentedly began to crawl in the opposite direction, dragging one leg more than the other but very effectively managing to manoeuvre herself. She looked up at the visitor and smiled. Her father got down on her level and called to her again, arms outstretched. She turned herself into a sitting position to face him and stayed where she was, beaming at him.

The feeling of being in charge of where you go must be wonderful. Then the world gets bigger. It seems to matter less how you get around than the fact that you do. Another father affectionately talked about his son having recently joined the Ministry of Funny Crawls. More of a bottom-shuffling exercise, but very quick and effective. Often children will prefer to crawl quickly rather than struggle with walking and keeping their balance. Others will stand up proudly, master of all they survey, but not attempt to put one foot in front of the other. Others will insist on a finger to hold on to. Is this just a physical thing, to do with keeping balance? Or is it also to do with the security of your special grown-up close by as you are taking those first steps into a more distinctly separate, independent life?

The process of learning to walk and feeling confident enough for those first steps is psychological as well as physical. It is another very major emotional leap, full of conflict for the baby. There is clearly only one way forward, but something is inevitably being left behind. How wonderful to walk, but is your baby walking away from being a babe in arms? Your baby may need to come back to you again and again for hugs and reassurance as he or she starts to take these first steps. In fact it may be at precisely the time when babies are walking and striking out so confidently on their own that they are also, conversely, more clingy at times.

Building up confidence

It can often feel bewildering when the confident baby of that very morning has clung onto your skirt or trouser leg all afternoon. But this is natural. Despite how bold your one-year-old seems at times, one year is still a very young age. Your baby can build in confidence only through repeated experiences of moving away from you, returning for reassurance and finding it in you, and then moving away again. He or she will rely on a parent or carer to be there at all times, a solid rock, who can help them physically and emotionally to deal with life and what it has brought to them at that moment. Movements towards independence are experimental but the more success at this stage, the more confident your baby will become.

What seems to be needed is for your baby to somehow carry your encouraging voice with him or her on short journeys away from you. This encouraging internal voice can then sustain babies emotionally and give them the courage to strike out on their own small journeys – to let go of your hand and explore a flowerbed in the park, or to approach another child in the library, and so on. Again, being sensitive to your baby, being confidently supportive but going at his or her own pace seems to be what encourages them along.

Eryl's mother had taken him and his four-year-old sister to meet up with some close friends and their children. Most of the other children were nearer to his sister's age, whereas Eryl was just 17 months. It was a sunny day and the older children ran into the garden while the mothers sat together by the open French doors. Rather unusually Eryl left his mother's side to join the children. It was the first time he appeared to be staking out his place as part of the children's group and all the adults commented on it. However, his mother also noticed that whereas the other children did not come inside for the next half-hour, Eryl would return and make some brief contact with her every five minutes or so, before venturing back outside with renewed confidence.

Inside your own home your one-year-old is likely to be even more adventurous. As soon as he or she learns to get around in a serious way, nothing will ever be the same again. Your baby's environment will probably need baby-proofing and this can feel like a major operation. From Peter's point of view, what really needed to be protected now, and kept out of Christine's reach, were his toys. Small babies are one thing, but moving one-year-olds are quite another. Luckily the entertainment factor generally balances out the equation and older siblings can have more fun with one-year-olds as they get older. But it is incredible how many potential safety hazards there may be in a home and if a parent does feel worried about safety, it's so much easier to do the baby-proofing quickly and comprehensively rather than running yourself ragged trying to keep tabs on your baby (crawling or toddling in the fast lane). The other option is to try to teach your baby not to go into that particular cupboard, or to pull a glass vase down from the shelf. But then you may find yourself saying "No" almost constantly and there are big drawbacks to this.

Marie's mother always tried to provide her with a collection of interesting toys to play with. But when they were in the kitchen, no matter how many of Marie's current favourites were selected for her, she always crawled over to a particular cupboard where she proceeded to take out every kitchen utensil, much to her mother's concern and exasperation. She found she was saying "No" to Marie time after time in the course of a day and rushing over to put things away. Marie would get fed up and frustrated too and couldn't be persuaded by her mother to play with anything else. Eventually, after talking it over with a friend, her mother decided she would fill "Marie's cupboard" with kitchen things that were safe for her to play with and that didn't matter being strewn all over the floor. Every so often she would put a new item in the cupboard, just for variety. This new arrangement worked much better for them both.

We have already talked about how empowering it is for your baby to learn to say "No". This may be particularly the case when they are so small and limited in what they are able and allowed to do for themselves. But as a one-year-old and growing child there will be many times when it is absolutely necessary and helpful for you to say "No". Even so, being on the receiving end of "No" can be very frustrating and belittling. Parents and carers often recognize this and so try to limit saying "No" only when it is really necessary.

Baby-proofing your home means your baby can explore it safely, as Marie was subsequently able to, building up her confidence. You will have to say "No" far less frequently and everyone can relax more.

There is also a psychological reason for saying "No" to your one-year-old only when you really need to. The first explorations of the home have a deeper significance than what just happens to be in the cupboard. Your baby's world is extending further as he or she is able to be more physically adventurous. If curiosity is alive and active then your baby will want to know as much as possible about your home and everything in reach within it. A curious mind is one that is growing and developing in the right direction – parents don't want to say "No" to that.

2

The Value of Exploration

Getting to know mother and then the wider world

The first important relationship a baby has is with the mother. This relationship begins even before birth as the baby grows inside her. At this point, she is the one who sustains life itself. Once born, it gradually becomes possible for the baby's mind to formulate questions about anything at all. Quite naturally the mother becomes the very first object of fascination and curiosity. The intense quality of this first relationship between baby and mother thrives on how endlessly curious the baby can be about her. One can imagine the kinds of questions: What is mother like on the inside? How do her breasts come to be full of milk? How does she feel right now? What is in her mind and heart? Who does she love? Who looks after her? And so on. If this kind of intense curiosity can be tolerated, without too much worry, by mother and baby, then the baby will feel confident to take such curiosity even further.

As a one-year-old, the world is getting bigger. Whether walking or crawling, there are more opportunities for independent exploration. What first began as a fascination with everything about mother can now be transferred into a fascination and curiosity in everything else. Parents and carers who can encourage this curiosity are at the same time supporting their one-year-old's emotional and psychological development – helping them to move on and engage with enthusiasm in the wider world. They are helping their child towards a secure, independent life. But the process can be complicated.

Some mothers can find it hard to lose the intensity of the early mother–baby relationship and they may experience their baby's growing independence as a personal slight, as if the baby did not care about them so much any more. This can especially be the case with the youngest child in a family, perhaps the "last" baby in the mother's mind. The baby may sense the mother's pain about this and respond by not being as adventurous as he or she might be under different circumstances, or by holding on to particular kinds of babyish ways and mannerisms.

It can also work the other way round, with some mothers coming into their own as their baby becomes increasingly independent, resulting in the mother–baby relationship positively deepening at this point. Orishe's mother, for instance, talked about how she wasn't really a "baby-person". She felt unconfident and became depressed staying at home. She returned to work as quickly as possible and with some relief when Orishe was a few months old, having found childcare she was very happy with. Things improved from here on. Now, some time later, Orishe was a more independent one-year-old and his mother felt very different – much more confident, and she spoke of really enjoying being with him. In fact it had recently become possible for her to reduce her working hours and she was looking forward to spending more time at home with Orishe, taking him to playgroups and so on.

If your one-year-old can be encouraged to explore the wider world, while still feeling secure in your love and attention, then he or she will grow more confident in further explorations and this will inevitability start with an exploration of the home. We have already talked about "baby-proofing" your house and how safety concerns are not the only reason why this may be important. If babies keep hearing "No" when all they are doing is following their increasingly healthy inclination for curiosity, they may become over-anxious about where their curiosity leads or even begin to feel so inhibited that they call a halt to their curiosity altogether. As such curiosity in the wider environment links into the development of the mind, parents and carers have endless opportunities for encouraging their baby's potential curiosity as far as it can go.

Working through feelings in the arena of play

Playing is good for children; it's fun. Playing with your baby – whether you are a parent, grandparent, aunt, uncle, family friend or childcarer – can be great fun too. Play is a wonderful arena in which curiosity and imagination can thrive and develop. It is also a place where many feelings and experiences can be dramatized and worked through. Very small children tend to play close to their mothers or carers. They tend to play in short bursts at first and often need an adult to refer to – to check in with at regular intervals – as a reassuring presence. Some gentle encouragement to take a game further may help, although your one-year-old will be able to set the pace that feels right so that the play does not escalate into an area that feels too overwhelming or goes too fast. An adult sensitive to this can do much to facilitate and create an environment conducive to the development of imaginative play.

A friend of Alan's mother visited the family around the time of his first birthday. She brought a gift for Alan – a group of four brightly coloured farm animals that rather dramatically popped up when the right button was pressed. Everyone tried to engage Alan in playing with his new toy, emphasizing the surprise element of the popping up animals with many exclamations of delight. But the friend noticed Alan's gaze in a different direction and thoughtfully handed him the box the toy had come in. To her amusement, Alan was clearly much more delighted with this part of the gift, turning the box over and over in his hands and studying it carefully before devising his own game of filling and emptying the box with bits of wrapping paper.

A familiar joke at many one-year-olds' birthday parties is that the baby prefers playing with the box the present came in rather than the present itself. Containers of all kinds seem to hold a deep fascination for children of this age and there are endless containers around to attract them. They are drawn to them like magnets and often become preoccupied with filling them up and emptying them out for investigation. The "childlock" on video players testifies to this, as do the myriad of small objects regularly found inside these machines when they go wrong.

Denise's mother was settling her daughter down to watch her favourite video one afternoon, and rather looking forward to the prospect of a possibly uninterrupted cup of tea herself, when to their mutual shock and consternation it was discovered that the video player had stopped working. Denise's mother quickly arranged for the video repair man to come and he arrived soon afterwards. Spotting Denise as he walked in the door, he went straight to the machine, turned it upside down and shook it, emptying out a collection of coins, small toys, a miniature screw driver and a radiator bleeding key. He then explained how the "childlock" worked, said he was used to all this, and left a few minutes later.

Another "container" that one-year-olds seem drawn to is the washing machine. Ella's mother first noticed her interest as Ella began to make regular trips to the washing machine during the course of a day, often carrying something and returning empty handed. She seemed especially fond of putting her milk bottle in there. Once the family had identified Ella's washing-machine game, the washing machine became the first place to look when anything went missing, particularly helpful on the occasion when no one could find the car keys and Ella's mother needed to get to work.

Whereas the baby's first fascination is his or her mother and all she contains in her heart, mind and body, this now progresses to something more symbolic of that in a fascination with containers in general. Finding a container or a containing space and putting things inside it seems to be a baby's way of exploring the potential safety of the world. If the container and its contents can be investigated and played with, then the play may help to reconfirm and reassure the baby about the capacity of strong, safe containers in general. A strong container could keep the good milk bottle safe, representing a good, feeding mother, and also, when needed, contain negative feelings about a Mummy who has a life at work away from the children. This kind of play transfers into a hopefulness about life and encourages the idea of a strong, protective figure who can know about and contain all the baby's feelings – both positive and negative. If your baby can develop this idea and root it securely in his or her mind, it will make all the difference to how the baby approaches the inevitable trials and tribulations of life ahead.

The feel of your baby's play can vary tremendously, not only day to day and week to week, but also moment by moment. Playing with your baby and paying close attention to following his or her lead can help you to understand something about the baby's current feelings and preoccupations as they are spread out before you in the drama of the game. Sometimes the arena of play can feel more like a Roman arena – crashes, disasters and destruction all around – and adults may look on rather horrified and feel tempted to stop the game in the interests of "playing nicely". In fact, imaginative games are often an opportunity to work through very passionate, difficult feelings and experiences and they can work towards putting the baby back in touch with a more hopeful state of mind.

Nana's father, who had been under a lot of pressure at work, was looking after his small daughter as she began to walk at around 14 months. She was, as yet, still quite wobbly on her feet. She lost her balance a number of times as she crossed the sitting room to give a family friend toys and her drink to hold. Eventually she handed her father her toy dog on wheels and wanted him to untangle the string for her. As he was working on this he watched Nana start playing with some Duplo that had been constructed by her sister earlier. She picked up a small Duplo figure and balanced it on a wall of Duplo, apparently inadvertently knocking it down moments later. A Duplo pram was then examined carefully, with Nana touching the wheels. She took another Duplo figure out of its bed and tried to fit it into the pram. Finally, finding the figure was too big, she carefully replaced it back in the bed. She continued to play in this way, picking up all the figures and then carefully putting them back in the beds.

Nana seemed to show her concern that everything, like her toys and her drink, should be in a safe place, carefully held and contained. This could link to her own falling and a need to feel safe and held, more balanced physically and emotionally. The pressures on Nana's father may have echoed her own feelings of precariousness and made her need to be a safe baby even more pressing. Despite this, she was able to identify her father as the Daddy who could untangle and make things run smoothly – a protective figure in her mind. Her play with the Duplo showed her working through and processing her feelings and the outcome in the game was good. Despite there being some falling down, as the first figure fell from the wall, eventually all the figures found a safe place to be.

Different kinds of families

Families are different in many ways. In some families both parents are living together with the children. Other families have single parents and the emotional and practical support of an extended family, while some single parents rely more on a close network of friends or local services. However the group is made up, each family has its own culture, its own history and its own way of thinking about children.

All families undergo periods of strain at different times; this is part of life. The pressures may be emotional or financial: the marriage may be in difficulty; one of the parents may have left the family; there may be a bereavement or a long-term illness to cope with; unemployment could be a problem; work commitments could mean long periods of absence from home; remarriage of a parent or the arrival of a new baby could introduce changes and mixed feelings, and so on. Whatever it is, children are never immune to what is happening in their family, even when they are too young to put their feelings into words. This can often be a very painful realization for parents who have, above all, wanted to protect their children. But, in fact, recognizing that family issues will affect all its members, and so allowing yourself to be in touch with

your child's experience, is the first step towards helping him or her to emotionally digest any painful or confusing feelings.

Thinking about your child's experience will help to contain and support
him or her emotionally. For pre-verbal children this kind of thoughtful adult
containment is essential to help them deal with a crisis in the family. They are
not mature enough to emotionally digest problems on their own and their
uncontained distress will inevitably spill out in other ways – behaviour,
eating, sleeping, bed-wetting, physical symptoms and so on. Young children
who have some words may want to talk about the problem. Being open and
receptive to this is not a question of going into details with your child, especially when the problem essentially involves adult concerns. Young children
are not helped by knowing the ins and outs of financial difficulties, details of
marital disagreement or blow-by-blow accounts of a parent's or sibling's
illness. But a simple, honest presentation of the situation could do much to
unburden them. At the very least they may be helped by an adult acknowledg-
ing that they are worried and concerned about what is happening at home.
Then the way is open for them to talk or ask questions if they are able to.
During such times, some families find another perspective helpful and will
often contact their general practitioner (GP) who can refer to local services for
a few meetings of under fives counselling or support for parents.

David's mother got in touch with her GP when he was 18 months old and
bedtimes and sleeping were becoming intolerable. The GP made a referral to a
local under fives counselling service that offered up to six weekly sessions.
Over the weeks their story unfolded. David had become used to sleeping with
his mother after his father left the family six months earlier. From the start
David's father regularly saw him at weekends and they had a close relationship. At home David's mother struggled with trying to get David into his own
bed at bedtime. The only way he would be persuaded was if she lay down next
to him and pretended to go to sleep too. The whole process could take up to
two hours. When he woke later in the night he would get into bed with his
mother and by this time she felt too exhausted to move him back to his own
room. The broken nights were taking their toll on this family and mother said
she often felt depressed with little energy. However, as David's mother talked
about the situation at home, things seemed to become slightly easier. David
especially joined in the conversations about Daddy, showing he had clear
memories of what happened the night he left. His mother said she was
amazed as this was the first time he had said anything about it. What also
emerged during the sessions was how worried David was about his mother

leaving home too. After all, if Daddy could leave, why not her? He needed to keep an eye on her, particularly at night-time. This made going to bed especially difficult and of course he wanted to check up on his mother when he woke in the night. Once this was more in the open, David was able to be reassured by his mother and night-times became much better for the family.

As well as being responsible for day-to-day childcare, single parents will have the ongoing issue of their children living with only one of their natural parents and how this impacts on family life. If the relationship between the parents has ended, it is often an acutely painful time for all involved. After a while it may be possible for the parents to think and work together as a parental couple even when their personal relationship has broken down and they are no longer living together. If this can happen, it is clearly better for the children, who can then witness their parents successfully working together in their best interests. This is very reassuring for young children as it strengthens the network of support and emotional containment around their lives.

When a beloved partner has died, a single parent is left responsible for the children at the same time as desperately missing and needing to mourn for their loved one. With very young children involved, it can feel heartbreaking. Extended family and friends can do much to support single-parent families in these circumstances and a good memory of the parent who has died can strengthen and sustain the one raising the couple's children. A parent's capacity for holding a good memory in mind can extend to the children who are likewise held, contained and reassured by a united parental couple in their minds.

The idea of a united couple

The idea of a thoughtful, creative and united couple is very important for children. As an idea it is symbolic of the parents together, creative in their capacity to make a baby, strong enough to stay united in adversity and able to continue thinking creatively about the children. Even when the external parents have not stayed together, either personally or in their parenting – or possibly are living together but not in a creative, enriching way – the idea of the couple can still very helpfully be encouraged in children's minds. A grandmother, uncle, aunt or friend who is seen as supportive can also form part of a couple, and the idea can be strengthened in the child's mind from there. Sometimes a doctor, teacher or childcare worker will be recognized by the child as supportive of their parent, and this will reinforce the idea of a helpful couple. At the same time, if the single parent has an idea of a united couple in his or her mind, perhaps from their own childhood or subsequent life experience, then this will be transferred to the child too. Wherever a good link can be made and passed on, it will be useful.

So why is this idea of a good couple so important for children? It is really to do with encouraging their own potential to make good links and their own capacity to be creative. If they have an idea of what a good link is, represented by the united couple, then, with this model in mind, they will be able to make good links themselves. It will allow and encourage them to link with people through relationships in their own lives. It will also encourage their own creative thinking – making links in their own minds, putting thoughts together to form their own ideas. Being able to make good links is essentially a creative process.

Other things can get in the way of establishing the idea of a united couple in mind. This is an issue for all families and it is more to do with your child's own frustration with the idea.

Jennifer's parents were in the middle of redecorating their new home and there was a feeling of hopefulness in their united approach to the task. Jennifer's father had been looking after her while her mother was upstairs getting on with the wallpaper stripping. Father was supervising tea and Jennifer had just requested her third pot of fromage frais, dangling her full spoon provocatively over her shirt as if she was testing how far she could go before her father would tell her to stop. In between spoonfuls she engaged her father in naming things around the kitchen and was very giggly and attentive to him. After a while he told her he was just going upstairs to see Mummy and check on the wallpaper stripping.

When her father left the room, Jennifer began playing with her toy farm. She picked up a baby in a pram and said, "Ickle baby in pram, ickle baby," and put the pram on to the green farm board. She then took a small lorry, turning its wheels before running it right off the board in a wide circle. "There it goes," she said, leaving it on the carpet. She did the same thing, using the same words, with the pram, and then leaned over and retrieved the lorry. She began turning it over in her hands and putting her fingers inside. She put one finger very deep in the lorry and her expression became worried. "Stuck," she said. Father returned, helped her get her finger out and kindly warned her against doing it again.

Jennifer seemed identified with the "ickle baby in pram" now that her father was with her mother. She may have projected her wish – "I want all of

Mummy" – on to the parental couple and as a result their union would mean no room for her. In this situation she could only feel like the left out, excluded little baby. The lorry – "There it goes" – seemed to represent her parents together, soon followed by the "ickle baby" in the pram. Jennifer demonstrated how she wanted to intrude when she poked her fingers deep into the lorry. When she got worried and needed help, her father was there to save her, and set a boundary for her at the same time.

The idea of parents together can leave your child feeling small, helpless and excluded. Especially when children are very young they can want all of their mother, to the exclusion of everyone else, and this idea leaves little space for the idea of a united couple in the child's mind. Yet if the reality is that father is emotionally strong enough to shoulder the seeming rejection and still remain friendly to the child and protect the mother from the endless demands of the children, all will turn out for the best.

Later, the one-year-old little girl may become fixated on Daddy and want to be his partner. She can feel torn between her wish to exclude Mummy from the picture altogether and her love and need of her mother. Similarly the one-year-old little boy may not only admire and identify with his father but also want to get rid of him and usurp him in Mummy's affections, so coming between the parental couple in his mind. These kinds of Oedipal phantasies are part of childhood experience. You will see them in your child's play, you will feel them as a parent in many different circumstances. In single-parent families when there is not the external reality of parents together to contradict the phantasy, recognizing your child's dilemma and continuing to encourage the idea of a good couple in his or her mind is very valuable. Of course, it is reassuring for children when they feel that external reality contradicts their phantasy and the parents remain together and united in their approach. But this does not always make the problem go away. It is an ongoing struggle for young children and is not necessarily resolved in childhood.

Sometimes parents can find the Oedipal situation very difficult and it can put families under enormous strain. Everyone has been a baby once and unresolved Oedipal feelings of rivalry with your demanding young child are common. However, for some parents such feelings can be overwhelming. Parents in this position may need to take stock and get help to keep the family together. Parents committed to facing the challenge together still have a great deal of work. Single parents either get external support from a strong figure who can help them set boundaries for the children, or depend on the resources within themselves, linked to their own idea of a united parental couple. Some circumstances require single parents to try to function both as mother and father in one person, providing the love, care and understanding at the same time as setting boundaries and limits to help contain the children emotionally and practically. Parenting is hugely demanding, whatever way you look at it.

Family meals

The family meal is often regarded as the epitome of family life. It can be a time when everyone comes together – all with their own needs – and, even on the simplest occasions, there is an emotional investment in the meal going well. Of course, this in itself brings its own pressures and family meals that can sometimes be a real pleasure at other times can become emotionally charged.

Integrating your one-year-old into some family meals probably started a while ago, when he or she began eating solid food. By the age of one children could be eating more or less the same food as everyone else but many tastes and textures will still be a novelty to them. Very young children seem to enjoy spreading their food around. In the interests of a tidy mealtime and clean baby, it may be tempting to always feed him or her yourself. But exploring food more independently, and getting some in their mouth along the way, helps youngsters to get used to new tastes and textures on their own terms and a bit of mess at this stage could mean a more adventurous eater later on. If toleration levels are fairly high, family meals can become a more interesting and varied experience with a one-year-old at the table.

If your one-year-old is a "good eater" then mealtimes are probably not too much of an issue in the family. But if you are worried about your one-year-old's eating then mealtimes can feel very stressful.

Jade's mother found every mealtime a worry. Jade had always been slightly underweight and was never enthusiastic about food from the start of her weaning and introduction to solid food. Her mother was concerned about her weight and felt that every mealtime was crucial. If things didn't go well, the meal could turn into a battle of wills which then often ended in tears. Feeling rather desperate about the situation, Jade's mother tried to think about the problem in the context of Jade's whole personality. She felt that she had always been a baby who didn't like overwhelming situations. She would cry if a stranger's face came too close to her too quickly or if she felt thrust into anything unfamiliar. Large, noisy crowds or excited parties frightened her and she preferred a routine where she felt more in control and knew what was coming next. Thinking about food in this context, Jade's mother tried a different approach. She prepared only finger food for a while and began offering just tiny amounts to Jade so as not to overwhelm her. With this new approach, Jade seemed more interested and would ask for more, again given to her in very small amounts – a few peas, two pasta shapes and so on. Over the course of the mealtime, she began to eat far more than she had done when the food was presented to her all in one go.

Despite her own worry, Jade's mother was able to contain Jade emotionally. Her thoughtfulness – linking Jade's emotional reaction to feeding with her own understanding of Jade's personality – and the creativity of her fresh approach shifted what had felt like a very stuck situation for them both. But it is not always easy to do this.

The whole area of feeding is full of emotional significance for mothers and babies. In the womb babies are nourished solely through their mothers. It is a baby's relationship of complete dependency on the mother and the mother's gift. It is a question not only of the baby's healthy growth but also one of life or death – survival itself. Once born, mothers will continue to feed with the same mindset, either through breastfeeding or by using bottles. And to a certain extent, the relationship of dependency still dominates the feeding. As the baby is weaned and goes on to solid food, he or she is gradually moving towards a more independent position, but one still emotionally loaded with feelings of dependency.

Dependency is a tricky issue. It can be hard to feel so dependent on others. Yet it is something we are all born into as we are all dependent on our parents for our existence. There is the utter dependency on our mothers in utero. Then, as tiny babies we are dependent for our continued life on the adults around who care for us. And then... The list of favours that confirm and reconfirm our condition of dependency is endless – there is no escaping it. Yes, we know in our minds that this should all make us feel endlessly grateful, but it often just makes us feel grumpy and cross (as well as grateful).

As a one-year-old, things have undoubtedly moved on. Crawling or walking, maybe beginning to talk – this is a far cry from the helpless newborn. But your one-year-old is still dependent on you for so much day-to-day care. Of course there is the small issue of the nappies. But this is nothing in comparison to your one-year-old's emotional dependency on you. Being in touch with your baby's mixed feelings about dependence, and the crossness with you involved in this, is now part of your task in containing him or her emotionally. Finding opportunities that allow one-year-olds some mastery over their environment helps them stomach all the rest. In fact, food –

something so emotionally linked to dependency – is one of the few areas where one-year-olds are now able to assert themselves and make a choice rather than being totally dependent on their carers' choice. And with choice comes power.

Ben loved it when the family went to stay at his grandmother's. He got lots of attention and his grandmother always made a point of getting in his favourite foods. With Ben's mother being allowed a lie in, breakfast was a special time between Ben and his grandmother. They both enjoyed it immensely, with his grandmother proudly calling Ben a "breakfast man" and breakfast being his "best meal of the day". Throughout the visit they would establish a breakfast routine – cereal, toast, fruit and lots of it. She always asked him what cereal he wanted, hoping it might be the same as last time he visited, but each visit Ben had changed his mind about what his latest cereal passion was. Did his grandmother insist he finished the last packet first? A long row of different cereals in her larder told the rest of the story, as did Ben's very good mood after breakfasts with Gran.

These small choices can empower one-year-olds, allowing them to recognize their own agency in the world, despite their dependence on you. This is completely different from feeling controlled by your child over food, or running yourself ragged trying to prepare different meals for different children. Obviously a balance needs to be struck so that children can make choices while the adults stay in charge. But being indulged as the "breakfast man" at least meant Ben felt in charge of breakfast, even if his one-year-old dependency meant he couldn't be in charge of very much else. It was a good start to the day and such good experiences help to build up the idea of an encouraging figure or couple in one's mind. Ultimately it is the ongoing dependency on this good idea that will help your one-year-old through life.

3

Emerging Personality

Finding one's own identity

As one-year-olds grow, their unique personality will begin to emerge more clearly. With increased mobility and a few words they are now better able to make their presence felt in the family. Each time they assert themselves is another opportunity to develop their own sense of identity, find out for themselves what kind of person they are. There may also be some experimentation at this stage – trying on the identities of different kinds of characters and seeing what they feel like. This journey of discovery is crucially important; babies need to find their own way in order to be their own person. And babies, like people, do things differently.

Some mothers were chatting about their one-year-olds and how they were when they woke up in the morning. One mother talked about how her daughter would wake in her cot and usually play with her toys for at least half an hour before anyone needed to go to her. Her parents could hear her laughing and talking to her toys over the baby monitor. Another two mothers, incredulous at this story, talked about how their children would cry piteously to be taken out of their cots the minute they woke up. The last mother said her daughter didn't do either of these things. What she did was wake up and *shout* at the top of her lungs until someone went to her. The sound was so deafening it usually didn't take long.

Some children will thrust themselves on their families with great gusto at this time. Others will be more tentative and may need encouragement to assert themselves. Whatever the case, the important thing is that the lead comes from your baby rather than your baby fitting into someone else's mould.

This situation can happen without anyone in the family really being aware of it. Sometimes a child can resemble a relative and the likeness is so strong it's hard to see the person in front of you. It could be that a loved family member has died and your one-year-old, in some way, replaces that person in the family's mind. When your child begins to assert his or her own personality, it may be more difficult to recognize as it is different from the person "replaced". Young children asserting themselves outside of the expected mould could come as a shock that disturbs the family and upsets the status quo. Sometimes in these circumstances children are inhibited, unable to express themselves as they really are, being aware at some level that their life is not their own.

A similar situation can arise if parents' hopes for their child become too muddled with what they had hoped for in their own lives. Sándor Márai describes this in his novel *Embers* (1942). A young musician, serving in the army, talks about his life and sees that from early childhood he has been unrecognized as a person. This is despite the fact that his parents sacrificed a great deal for him – for his education and lifestyle. He believes he became his parents' "masterpiece" but at the same time disconnected from himself and what could breathe real life and music into his being.

Recognizing your baby for who he or she is fosters the development that helps them feel they are themselves, rather than a shadow of someone else or someone else's ambition. Only if they are themselves can they go on to reach their potential, whatever that potential may be. And this begins in the family. But who you are in the family depends to a certain extent on where you are placed in the family. Whether your one-year-old is the first child, the only child or has older brothers or sisters will make a difference.

Your baby's place in the family

If your one-year-old is the first child then he or she will probably have had more of your attention than if there are older brothers or sisters in the family. This is obviously beneficial in some ways: it is a special thing to have your parents' attention all to yourself. Physical achievements will be quickly noticed and rejoiced over; first words may be spoken to a hushed, focused audience; first experiences will be firsts for everyone in the family and they will be treasured because of it. From an emotional point of view, being an oldest child could have other benefits. Your one-year-old may have to contend with jealous feelings when younger brothers or sisters come along but will at least have worked through and survived this experience in childhood. Such previous experience in itself could help in later life in the approach to other relationships with similar feelings.

If your one-year-old will be the only child in the family then he or she will have some of the benefits of first children, and may also relax easily and comfortably in adult company, having had the advantage of a lot of interested adult conversation. Parents of only children will often make a big effort to arrange regular playdates with their child's friends so they can mix with their peers too. This is obviously helpful as well as being fun for your child.

If your one-year-old is already part of a family of brothers or sisters, there will be different issues to contend with. Growing up as part of a larger family has its benefits too. Being able to witness the rough and tumble of family life provides endless entertainment and stimulation. It's true that your one-year-old may have to contend with the jealousy of older siblings but, with luck, they could also become friends to play with and practise that famous childhood game called "Learning to be Civilized". Certainly learning to share and being part of a group may be less of an issue if your baby has been used to these things from early on.

A newborn baby in the family

Your one-year-old does not have to wait for the new baby to be born in order to feel ousted by this interloper.

Julie, coming up to her second birthday, was generally not a bad sleeper but over the last month or so had been coming to her mother a number of times a night and making a fuss about being taken back to her own room. She had also been unusually clingy to her during the day. Her mother was seven months pregnant at the time and Julie's nightly wanderings felt like a real blow. One morning she tried to talk to Julie about it, telling her that she really needed to sleep in her own room and not be with her mother all the time. At this Julie burst out "Baby with Mama all the time!"

Momentarily shocked by Julie's eloquence, her mother could then suddenly and vividly see things from her small daughter's perspective. While Julie had to tolerate saying goodnight at bedtime and cope with many other small separations from her mother during the day – going into another room in the house, being on the telephone, and so on – this unborn baby got to stay with Mama constantly, held inside her womb every second of the day and night. Looking at it this way, it felt painfully unfair. Julie's mother was now able to talk to her daughter about this, put her experience into words for her and so contain the painful experience. In this way Julie could be emotionally held and contained. It was a different kind of holding than the way her mother held her unborn baby, but it was a holding that would keep Julie safe and secure in her mother's understanding.

Julie and her mother continued these kinds of conversations as the pregnancy progressed and so her mother was able to be in touch with Julie's many conflicting feelings about the new baby. Being able to put her feelings into words and have her hostility recognized would have done a lot to contain Julie, and it gave her mother the opportunity to reassure her. A few weeks before the baby was due to be born they were talking about where the baby would sleep. Julie had already seen the Moses basket in evidence. The more tricky question was going to be where it would go. Julie suggested that the garden would be a good place. It took a while to persuade her otherwise, but it was also another opportunity to discuss how Julie worried that the baby would take over all the available space in the house when he was born. Her particular worry was that there wouldn't be enough of Mama to go round.

These kinds of conversations, before the baby is born, will certainly help your one-year-old. It is also important that your child knows in advance what the arrangements will be when the baby comes – who will be looking after him or her, when the one-year-old will be able to see his or her mother and the baby and so on. Perhaps, thinking in advance, it would also be helpful if on the first occasion after the birth, your arms were available for your one-year-old and you could then look at the new baby in the cot together.

Being heavily pregnant and coping with a toddler is an exhausting experience. One heavily pregnant mother was close to tears as she talked to her friend, saying that it was so difficult with her one-year-old now and if she wasn't managing now, how on earth could she manage with two children. Another mother, looking back on her experience, said she thought being heavily pregnant and looking after a todder was even more demanding than looking after two or three children once the baby had been born. The birth of a new baby in the family also brings great joy, and your one-year-old, with all his or her conflicting feelings, will feel very relieved to see the new baby alive and well.

If you are breastfeeding the new baby, this takes up an enormous amount of time and energy. Producing milk is physically demanding. Recognizing what you are demanding of your body means that you will also be trying to rest as much as you can, accepting all offers of support that are available.

Breastfeeding your baby in front of your one-year-old can also be a sensitive issue. Some children find the view of mother and baby in such intimate union very difficult. Your one-year-old may not be so far away from the experience of their own breastfeeding and seeing you feed the new baby may be a painful reminder that they are no longer at that baby stage. In such circumstances, feelings of wanting to be big can change very quickly into wanting to be little. Mothers can find themselves pulled in different directions, trying to breastfeed and at the same time trying to pacify a toddler who is upset and wanting attention. One also needs to think of the newborn baby and how he or she deserves to have some uninterrupted breastfeeding time with you.

Fathers can now come into their own and can do a huge amount to help and support their breastfeeding partner and their children – both practically and emotionally – as they will all inevitably be feeling sapped of energy at times and often vulnerable. For your one-year-old, having special times with Daddy will help to soften the blow of the time and attention Mummy needs to spend with the new baby. Single parents may find this period the most difficult of all. They will have all the physical demands of breastfeeding and all the emotions of their children to cope with. Trying to get help from family or friends so at least you can have some quiet uninterrupted feeds is a good idea. When this is not possible, settling older children with a drink of their own and maybe a biscuit and some activity that will hold their attention will help them to feel looked after and kept in their mother's mind too. Sometimes nothing works on these occasions. Don't despair. No one is superhuman and there is always the next time.

Respecting your baby's opinions, and when to say "No"

We have talked about how important it is that your one-year-old begins to assert him- or herself. Having one's own opinions, likes, dislikes and favourites are part of what makes you the person that you are. Parents may want to encourage this in principle while recognizing that the way ahead is paved with frustration – and not just for your baby. As babies begin to assert themselves in this way you need to recognize that some of their preferences may not be your own.

Jesecca enjoyed playing with dolls and had been given a number of beautiful dolls as presents. But it soon became clear that the doll she loved best was "Holiday Heidi". Heidi was beautiful in Jesecca's eyes but not in her mother's. Her mother often wished Jesecca could love a more tasteful doll but it was not to be. Heidi – garishly eager – went to every social occasion with them and Jesecca's mother learnt what it was to have a real child with her own opinions, rather than a doll.

Toys are only one of the areas where your one-year-old's opinions may challenge you. Food is another area: we have already mentioned the possibility of making some choices about food in the light of feelings of dependency around feeding. Just like any adult, your child will have preferences about food. Some tastes will appeal more than others and, within the context of a balanced diet, these likes and dislikes can be respected. Young children will understand that this does not mean that sweets and puddings can replace foods that help them grow in a healthy way, but that does not mean they won't try to get away with what they can. No young child should have to be sick in order to realize that too many sweet things are not good for them. There are times when saying "No" to your child is essential. Respecting your baby's opinions and respecting him or her as a person also means knowing the limits of a baby's experience and being prepared to draw the line at what is reasonable and in his or her best interests.

Some one-year-olds have very definite opinions about what clothes they like to wear. This is another area where, within reason, they can legitimately make some choices and assert themselves in a satisfying way.

Anish was never at a loss over what to wear. His mother recognized that he used clothes in a particular way – as a kind of armour that protected him against feelings of vulnerability – and was sensitive to how important it felt for Anish to make choices in this area wherever possible. He chose to wear clothes that made him feel strong and capable – a Bob the Builder sweatshirt was a favourite, as was a black Reebok top.

Anish always knew exactly what he wanted and it was usually at the bottom of a drawer of clothes. Of course this meant that everything else had to be taken out of the drawer first. This in itself could be frustrating for his mother but as choosing for himself seemed so important, she put up with it. However, when Anish started to slip off to his room and begin the search for *the* item himself, resulting in all the previously ironed and folded clothes regularly being scattered over the floor, relationships became strained. They needed to find a compromise. Anish's mother explained the problem to him – how *he* wanted to choose his clothes and *she* wanted to keep her good temper. She suggested it could work for them both only if she was there and he told her what clothes he wanted. Then she would get them. But he was *not* allowed to get his clothes out on his own – that messed them up. Anish agreed, and needed only occasional reminding.

Sometimes, however, it can feel as though nothing you say to your child makes any difference in terms of resolving a difficult situation between you. On these occasions there may be a fine line between one-year-olds asserting themselves and just making life difficult; what starts as one thing can turn into quite another. On some occasions, simply the practical business of getting your child dressed in the morning and out of the house can feel fraught with difficulty. You find yourself following your child around with a vest in your hand, looking for opportunities. Time is getting on, you don't want to be late for that appointment and your child seems to be doing everything he or she can to make things as difficult as possible. This kind of situation is so commonplace that perhaps it helps to remember that children are just sometimes like this, which is why looking after them is such hard work. It is almost as though the whole point of the stubborn behaviour is to wind you up in order to see how you deal with it. Why is this, and what on earth can you do about?

Parents have different ideas about how to control children. Some parents think that smacking is the final "No" and use this to discipline their children if they are going too far. But whereas every parent may have resorted to an involuntary slap in a moment of desperation, smacking as a regular way of disciplining your child is not helpful. It is not a thoughtful approach to bad behaviour and merely gives your child the message that the feelings behind his or her behaviour have produced a physical reaction in you, but have not been processed or contained by you in any kind of thoughtful way. End of story. But of course the story of your child's life goes much further and understanding, processing and containing your child's feelings are what will help him or her in the long run.

Going back to trying to understand the problem from a one-year-old perspective, the story continues to unfold. There are so many things you can do and your one-year-old can't. This infuriating situation is something children come up against again and again. They are still very young, so any time they can legitimately insist "Me do it!" and it works out for them, it will be a small but very important feather in their cap. Respecting your baby's legitimate achievements in this way and helping him to build on those achievements is a positive step towards helping children to develop a sense of respect in themselves.

Of course it will help babies develop respect for themselves if they feel you respect yourself too. Being able to say "No" to your child not only helps to

maintain a boundary for him or her that is in their best interests, but also recognizes your own limits as to what you will put up with in terms of treatment
and behaviour from your child. As a parent or carer of young children, these
limits will be stretched to their fullest extent. You will be tested on numerous
occasions and the tests will often be directed at areas where you feel at your
most vulnerable. You will put up with so much because you are dedicated to
raising your child up and this involves consistently making yourself available
to your child emotionally and absorbing and containing, on his or her behalf,
many of the frustrations your child will experience as part of growing up. But
for everyone there is a limit as to what they can take, and it is no bad thing for
your child to realize that people should not be pushed beyond their limits.
Respecting yourself in this way will be something that your child will also
come to recognize as the final "No".

Temper tantrums and fears

When a mother of a one-year-old asked an older, more experienced father
when his children started to have tantrums, he replied that as far as he could
recall they began before they were two years old and seemed to last a lifetime.

Another mother talked about her situation when she left a very successful
career in teaching to stay at home and look after her first baby, George. She
had been used to controlling classes of thirty adolescents and had been very
good at it. Then, one afternoon at home in the kitchen, George began to
scream, throw his food around and ended up in the classic bowl-on-the-head
position. George's mother described looking at her one-year-old and feeling
completely helpless, wondering "What should I do now?"

Your child having a tantrum can be a shocking and frightening experience. In the case of George and his mother the tantrum happened in the
privacy of their own home. When they happen in public, as often seems to be
the case, parents and carers have to endure the humiliation of onlooking
strangers as well as everything else. It's interesting that if your child does have
a tantrum in a public place then those who seem most intrigued by the whole
process tend to be other young children. They will often come close and gaze
transfixed at your screaming child, as if they are trying to work something out.
They may well be fascinated because they are so close to this same kind of precarious hold on balance in their own lives.

With the extreme feelings of dependency and the wish for control which
your one-year-old is prey to, holding everything in balance can be a very

insecure business. Sometimes the smallest thing can tip the balance and it is not the thing in itself but perhaps the culmination of everything on top of each other and all in the context of how hard it is to suffer being little and wanting to be big, or sometimes feeling overwhelmed by growing up and wanting to be little again. At last it is too much and your child will let rip – the floodgates have opened.

Nick's mother was in a toyshop with him and his older sister. They were choosing a birthday present for a friend. Nick became absorbed playing with a toy that lit up and whirred when he did something to it. When it was time to go he kept hold of the toy saying "Mine". His mother tried to talk him out of this idea, to no avail, and eventually she took the toy out of his hand, feeling that many pairs of eyes were on their ungainly tussle. This was the end for Nick. His furious screams filled the shop and he fought with his mother as she tried to put him back in his buggy, arching his back, slipping down the buggy and somehow managing to get a foot under a wheel as she tried to push the buggy out of the shop. Once again struggling with the buggy straps and a screaming Nick, his mother said she was shaking herself as she finally managed to get out of the shop.

The tantrum, in all its force, will usually be directed at the mother, but sometimes at a carer in her place. The adult's role is to act as a container for all the child's terrible, confusing, terrifying feelings. Your one-year-old depends on you to do this. Such extreme childhood feelings cannot be processed in any other way. But how do you react, or in the words of George's mother, "What do I do now?"

Many parents find the answer to this through trial and error and a more experienced parent will probably at least have an idea of what won't work. For example, parents soon realize that punishments like smacking just make things worse. Trying to reason with your child in these circumstances is also usually a non-starter as he or she is beyond all reason. Usually parents find that just holding their children, if they will let you, is the best thing. You could tell them you need to keep them safe and maybe say a few quiet soothing words to them until they have calmed down. You may, on the other hand, now be feeling so angry or upset yourself that it's better not to say anything until you feel calmer too. Nick's mother said she had to keep walking for some time until she felt calm enough to stop. It was only then that she could try to soothe Nick and calm him down too.

Your child will also be considerably shaken after having a tantrum. A father coming home at the end of a day like this can feel like a huge relief and

offer a welcome breathing space from the intensity of the mother–child relationship. A mother can also have a chance to be looked after and comforted.
Parents can then think together about what happened and what might be
behind the tantrum. A single parent will also need help at times like this.
Speaking to a good friend or relative will make a difference and if this does
not feel like enough, then looking for ongoing support from a counsellor or
parents' group may be helpful. The burden of this kind of day is often too
much to carry alone.

All children have had tantrums at some time or other. But if you feel it is
happening a lot, then you may want to think seriously about any ongoing
issues that could be affecting your child and possibly ask your GP for a referral
for help.

Later, when your child has recovered from the tantrum, you may be able to
talk about what happened and how difficult it was for him or her. It is likely
that your child will be most anxious about what this attacking tantrum has
done to you and he or she may express this by being clingy or fretful.
Showing your child that you are able to think about what happened, even if
you don't have all the answers, will reassure your child that you have survived
the attack and are still able to function as a container, strong enough to hold
even such extreme feelings.

Recognizing that their most extreme feelings can be contained by you is
very reassuring for your child. Uncontained feelings of this kind are experienced as very dangerous and come back to haunt young children. In fact, it is
these very same attacking, hostile, tantrum-like feelings that are behind many
of the irrational fears and phobias of childhood. They can attach themselves
to all sorts of rather mundane objects, animals or insects, and can be experienced by your child as an attack coming back at them. By now the attacking
feeling will have become disconnected from its original tantrum-like projection, and it will just be located in the thing that the child fears.

Isobel moved with her family to a new house when she was 20 months.
She seemed to settle down well, liked her new room and loved playing in the
new garden. Then, quite out of the blue, she became wary of the boiler in the
bathroom and would jump out of her skin when it made a noise. What started
off as a small worry progressively got worst until Isobel was refusing to go
anywhere near the boiler at all. She would scream, quite clearly terrified,
when her mother tried to take her in the bathroom for her evening bath.
Nothing her mother could say seemed to make any difference. Finally her
mother decided to give Isobel her "bath" in the kitchen sink for a while and

she used the time to talk to her more about the boiler, letting her know she recognized her fears and reassuring her that it would all be all right. Eventually Isobel's fear diminished and life resumed as normal.

In this kind of situation, as well as recognizing and containing your child's fear it will also be reassuring for the child to feel held by firm, consistent boundaries in his or her day-to-day life. Appropriate limits around children's own behaviour reassures them that their mother is protected from the worst of their hostile tantrum-like attacks. A mother and father together can be a good double act in this respect with the mother as the container and the father as the boundary keeper, setting appropriate limits for the children and essentially protecting mother from becoming overwhelmed. Again single parents may need to find it in themselves to function in both roles, or to enlist the help of a friend or relative. However it is achieved, if one-year-olds can feel held in an environment strong enough to contain even their most extreme feelings, they will become less anxious and these kinds of fears will diminish.

4

Having a Good Idea and Keeping It

Saying goodbye and saying hello

When babies are very small they will often cry even when their mother walks into a different room in the house. At this stage when mother is out of sight she is experienced as completely gone, leaving the baby feeling all alone. Gradually one-year-olds will not feel so anxious about this kind of thing. They will be aware when mother leaves the room but they will be able to hold on to their anxiety about this and they now have a certain amount of experience of mother returning so they are more likely to expect that. But they will continue to struggle with the experience of mother coming and going and will deal with the situation in different ways.

At 18 months Holly sat in her high chair after being fed, banging her empty cup on the table and saying "Gone". Then she said "Down" and was helped down by her mother. Once on the floor Holly did a little jump. "Ump," she said, smiling, and her mother echoed, "Yes, jump." When her mother left the room to run Holly's bath, Holly responded to her leaving by continuing to jump, saying "Ump" each time. She then picked up a balloon from the other side of the room, saying "Boon". With her finger she carefully traced the writing on the balloon, before throwing it to the floor and saying "Ump". She became very absorbed with this game, throwing the balloon down with increasing force. The last couple of times the balloon went down Holly said, "Mummy ump" with each throw.

Holly's game seemed to centre around her wish to be in control of her mother's comings and goings, rather than at the mercy of her being "gone".

The phantasy in the game changed the facts of reality that Holly found unpleasant. She changed the experience of being a little baby and her mother putting her down from her high chair to herself jumping, so taking full control of the situation in her mind. The balloon then became a Mummy that Holly could throw down and make to jump at will. In the game Holly is working through her feelings about separation from her mother, although at this stage she needs to be in control and so distances herself from the pain of feeling like the little girl left behind.

Sometimes one-year-olds will protest loudly when their mothers leave them with anyone else, even someone they know well like their father, grandmother or a trusted babysitter. Parents can worry unduly about this. But young children are just showing their mother how important she is to them and it is a natural thing to get upset when someone you love goes away. Young children need comforting at this time and an experienced babysitter will be able to do this. It would, of course, be more worrying if your baby consistently showed no reaction at all to your leaving. If this is the case, parents may wonder if something is preventing their one-year-old reacting to the separation in an ordinary way. It may be that the children feel under pressure to be unrealistically independent and are completely cutting themselves off from their feelings. If this way of coping with separation becomes too entrenched, it will not be good for your child in the long term. Children need to know that their painful feelings about separation can be openly expressed to the adults around. Then there is the possibility of having those feelings acknowledged and contained in a helpful way.

The value of brief separations

Brief separations are good for both one-year-olds and their parents. A mother can return after a few hours feeling revived and her baby will have the benefit of a mother revitalized. In those few hours your one-year-old will also have the opportunity of forming closer relationships with others that can be life enriching. As long as the period of time you are away is not too much for your baby to tolerate, he or she will also have the satisfaction of coping without you, surviving and enjoying the experience. Sometimes parents try to fit this into their weekly routine and the consistency of a familiar pattern of brief periods away can work very well.

Ann's mother organized weekly yoga classes for herself to coincide with a time when Ann's father could leave a little early from work and look after his daughter. This arrangement not only allowed Ann's mother some precious time to herself but also provided an opportunity for Ann and her father to develop a special routine of their own. After dropping Ann's mother off at the yoga class, Ann and her father would go home together on the "Big Red Bus", always stopping off at the same shop for Ann's current favourite treat – "Kisp". Such regular routines incorporate brief separations into your baby's life as well as providing a space for deepening important relationships. Your one-year-old will also feel more in control of the separation as it will be recognized as coming around in a regular pattern each week. Quite apart from anything else, Ann and her father enjoyed their time together.

Returning to work and finding the right childcare

Some mothers will have gone back to full-time work soon after the birth of their baby, either preferring to do this from their own point of view or doing so out of financial necessity. Others will want to be full-time mums for the foreseeable future, while others still will be thinking of going back to work part-time when their baby is around the age of one or two. If you are thinking of going back to work at some stage, the issue of childcare is a major concern in the family.

Unless you are lucky enough to have a relative who is close by and committed to help, the choices tend to be finding a nanny, an au pair, a childminder or a nursery. Parents make their childcare choice depending on their child's needs and what is available in their local area; and what is of a high standard in one area is not necessarily so in another. Parents will do their own research and talk to other families in the neighbourhood. When making this kind of choice parents are wanting what will be most helpful for their child at his or her stage of development.

Au pairs are usually quite young and often find the responsibility of looking after a one-year-old daunting, preferring to work alongside a mother or a more experienced carer in these circumstances. A qualified nanny will generally be more confident with this age group, having received specific training and often coming with previous experience. A childminder usually has the experience of bringing up her own family and can provide a family atmosphere for your child in her home, with a very small group of children of varying ages, all coming together rather like brothers and sisters. Nurseries can vary a great deal but an institutionalized environment will certainly be unfamiliar to your baby and may not meet his or her needs at this age.

Some nurseries may be particularly impressive in their efficiency, but efficiency is no substitute for warmth and affection and very young children are too little to cope with institutional life. One-year-olds need a specific, trusted adult to relate to, to contain their feelings and help them emotionally digest their experiences. This is more difficult to provide in an environment where children have to relate their needs to a group of staff rather than to one person. Having said this, some good playgroups and nurseries do have a specific "key worker" system where a helper is allocated to each child and the expectation is that the child will build a special relationship with that person. It is then a question of how well the system works.

Bearing all these things in mind, at this young age babies need a sensitive, thoughtful and warm carer while they are away from their mother – a containing figure who can keep them safe and help them manage the day until mother gets home. It is a very important job and looking for childcare can be extremely stressful and agonizing for parents, particularly mothers. Once the right care is found the relief is enormous.

Preparing your one-year-old for the new arrangements will now go a long way towards helping you both manage this separation. Introductions to the new person or environment, and time spent with you there too, will help your baby feel secure about anything new. Talking to your baby in a very simple way will also help. The important thing he or she needs to know is when you are coming back. It will also help if your baby sees you are confident that, even if he or she finds it hard to say goodbye, they will be all right. And then, with all the best laid plans made and all the preparations carefully worked through, don't be surprised if on your first morning back you find your car keys in the washing machine.

The pain of intimacy

The closer you get to love, the more you allow a person to know you and you to know them. The powerful intimacy of this can make you extremely vulnerable. You become deeply affected by their thoughts and feelings, their comings and goings. You depend on them. You are wide open to being hurt and frustrated and also feel responsible in relation to your loved one and what you may have done to hurt them. If the intimacy is too painful you may cut yourself off from your loving feelings, become indifferent or reject the idea of love and choose another goal in your life. If you do this, you are at once defended against the pain of intimacy, but you are left with a separate, rather more deadening problem. You have, in effect, cut yourself off from your own potential as a person and the possibility of engaging fully in intimate relationships.

A baby's relationship with his or her mother is deeply significant. It may be the first relationship in which true loving feelings are experienced and can be worked through. Such feelings are not dissimilar to those of an adult in love. As the young lover, your one-year-old does not have an easy way ahead. Not only are there feelings of helplessness and dependency to contend with, but also the frustration of separations. Your child gradually begins to recognize his or her mother as a separate person with real feelings and with this recognition comes more pain. One-year-olds have depended on their mother so much to be a container for all their feelings. They have needed this. But then comes the awareness of the burden that this has placed on the mother, what she has had to suffer on their behalf, and with this awareness comes fear and deep concern over the damage they have done. Love goes hand in hand with taking responsibility. And then, ultimately, heartbreak, as the idea of possessing mother totally is understood to be unrealistic and, let us hope, is replaced by the idea of a helpful parental couple.

Understanding your one-year-old involves appreciating something of the potentially searing quality of this love and the pain this involves for him or her. Babies of this age are not "too young to notice" what is happening around them, particularly when it relates to those they love. Their inexperience means that they are likely to become confused easily, but the passionate nature of their loving feelings is blatant.

Luca's mother talked about a difficult time in her life which coincided with the final few months of breastfeeding her one-year-old son. She described a time when, in the middle of a feed, her mind turned to her troubles and her mood naturally became low. Although she was sure she did not show him any outward signs of this, she was surprised to notice that Luca had stopped feeding and was craning his neck up to look directly into her eyes. His expression of deep concern amazed her, as did the way he studied her face and held her gaze. Only after she had smiled and talked to him a little would he continue with the feed.

Babies and young children, like Luca, can be very alert to their mother's moods and states of mind. Evidence of genuine lively feelings can come as a great relief and reassurance that, despite everything, their mother still has the emotional resources to look after the children. A mother who finds herself depressed for a longer period will need to see her GP. These are very difficult times but parents with young children often need to depend quite heavily on others for a while until they are able to get themselves back on their feet.

From your one-year-old's point of view, there is the ongoing issue of how to tolerate the intensity of their feelings of love and responsibility in the light of the frustration and pain of separations from their loved one. It is not a question of being able to completely protect them from these feelings. Such feelings are part of what it is to be human and engaged in the world. But by appreciating the extremity of much of what your one-year-old needs to endure, you will be helping him or her along the way. Having someone understand you and your pain makes a huge difference. It also helps build trust in the idea of a helpful figure or couple in your mind that can sustain you through inevitable separations and generally throughout life.

Developing trust

For one-year-olds to develop this kind of trust, they will need to start by developing trust in important figures in their lives, usually their parents. Perhaps particularly in some single-parent families this will include important figures in the extended family too. There are ways of helping your baby develop trust in you. One involves the way you manage separations.

Natasha's parents were concerned that their daughter, who was 22 months, was becoming very clingy. She didn't seem to want to let whichever parent was looking after her out of her sight. If they planned to leave her anywhere, for example in a crèche on a shopping trip, she seemed to catch wind of the idea beforehand (despite the fact that they were careful never to mention it) and she would get very edgy. At the point of going into the crèche she would usually start screaming. Natasha's parents got particularly worried about this as they had just started to leave her at a playgroup for a few hours three times a week. It was not going well.

Natasha's mother talked about how they would take Natasha to the playgroup and then slip out quietly when she seemed preoccupied with an activity like play-dough and wasn't looking. This had worked at first, although they had had to collect her early a few times when her very experienced and sympathetic key worker had been unable to console her. But recently when they were dropping her off she would hold firmly on to her parent's hand, even if she was playing with the play-dough with the other hand. Then, when they tried to go, she would scream so much that both parents, on separate occasions, hadn't the heart to leave her.

After talking things through with the key worker, and thinking more about Natasha's worries about separation, Natasha's parents decided to take a different approach. While she was settling into the new experience of playgroup, they tried to avoid leaving Natasha at other more unfamiliar crèches for the time being. They also began to prepare her in a simple, confident way beforehand, each time she went to playgroup. They told her they would stay five minutes, say goodbye for a little while, and later come back to say hello and take her home. Natasha, who was not yet talking, clearly understood this and would begin to cry. Her parents would be sympathetic but remain confident with her that she would be all right for a little while.

Natasha's tears beforehand, and her parents' opportunity to contain her worries at that time, seemed to have the effect of less panic at the moment of their departure from the playgroup. When they said goodbye, Natasha still protested very loudly and either parent would be sympathetic but confidently put her in the arms of the key worker as they left. Natasha began to recognize the routine of this and clearly felt more in control now that her parents said goodbye in a straightforward way. Developing more trust at that point seemed to help her trust that her parents would be there to collect her, like they said.

Within two weeks Natasha's parents were relieved to notice she was no longer being clingy. Her key worker reported that she stopped crying just a few minutes after her mother or father left and would get absorbed in an activity she enjoyed. She was also much more settled during her few hours at playgroup although her key worker noticed that she sometimes became anxious during transitions, when changing from one activity to another, and needed extra reassurance at this time to help her settle again. It seemed that being able to trust her parents with the goodbye routine helped Natasha to strengthen her sense of a trustworthy parental couple in her mind. This idea, combined with the thoughtful sensitivity of her key worker, seemed to keep her going while she was away from her parents.

There will always be times and situations which prompt your one-year-old to take a step back and need extra reassurance from a parent or carer. Sometimes this can happen just after there has been a new development forward and can feel quite baffling in the light of your baby's previous progress. But some swings between a more confident independence to feelings of insecurity and smallness are quite natural and will continue throughout childhood.

The sense of safety that routines can offer babies and young children should not be underestimated. It takes us back to the understanding of how much your baby needs to depend on others and how in this context established and recognizable routines lend a certain sense of predictability to life. If babies can feel something familiar about the structure of their day, they will feel more in control and less prey to anxious feelings about what might be around the corner. Of course, routines need to be flexible to allow everyone some freedom in family life, but for your one-year-old routines to do with meals, bath times and bedtimes will provide an environment of security. It will help to build your child's trust in what family life can provide and trust in a world where he or she is less at the mercy of the unknown.

A good night's sleep

Being able to sleep through the night is an achievement for babies and young children. Like feeding, it is one of the first things that tends to get disturbed if there is something that is worrying or upsetting your one-year-old.

It may also be helpful to think about falling to sleep as another kind of separation situation for your baby. It is a different kind of goodbye – this time a goodbye that needs to last through the night with all its unknowns. Your baby's worries about "falling" to sleep may be linked to an anxiety about being securely enough held in an emotional sense, or whether he or she could fall from your mind in the darkness of the night. It is really back to the question of trust.

The night, with all its potentially nightmarish elements, speaks quietly but clearly through the nursery rhyme song:

> Rock a bye baby, on the tree top,
> When the wind blows, the cradle will rock,
> When the bough breaks, the cradle will fall,
> Down will come baby, cradle and all.

On the face of it, this is not exactly reassuring. But perhaps the idea of a parent singing this as a lullaby, somehow encapsulating all the ghostly, precarious and unpredictable fears of the night in soothing tones, says more about a parent's capacity to emotionally contain and hold a child's night-time fears. Young children's wavering trust may link more to their own struggles to keep a secure hold on a helpful figure in their mind, rather than on their parents' actual capacity to hold them emotionally. Babies may need reassurance about the difference between themselves and their parents.

As a parent you may need to acknowledge openly night-time fears in your child. It may also help to recognize that, like other fears and phobias, they too probably stem from a projection of your child's original tantrum-like hostile feelings. When such feelings are so split off from their originator, it is very difficult to recognize them as anything to do with oneself. The original angry feeling has become transformed into an unrecognizable fear that is coming back to attack in the dead of night. But having the angry feeling understood as part of his or her own personality in the first place can go a long way towards diluting such fears and putting them into a more reasonable perspective.

A settling bedtime routine at the same time each night can also help your young child feel secure and emotionally held by you before going to sleep.

Annie's bedtime routine was one of the first things she talked about when she started using some words. She liked to predict what was coming next and while she was still in the bath she would ask for her "warm towel" that was always hung out ready for her on the radiator. A cup of milk and a bedtime story ended the day at 7 o'clock.

Spending some calm time with your baby at this stage of the day, doing simple, familiar things, helps him or her to feel relaxed and settled. Peter's and Christine's family had a bedtime routine that always included a plate of fruit with their bedtime story. After her bedtime story, Beatrice's mother always sang a lullaby. Different families have different routines, but the regularity of the same routine seems to be especially settling at bedtime.

Of course, even with routines no household is invariably an oasis of calm at bedtime. There may be the occasions when the towel gets thrown in the bath, the fruit squashed into the carpet and the lullaby drowned out by less melodious contributions. This is real life after all. But there is something about a helpful, familiar routine to fall back on, regardless of the mayhem that preceded it, that can hold your young child and the family together as well.

Thinking about toilet-training

Fashions change when it comes to ideas about toilet-training. The first question of debate seems to be when to start. Previous generations tended to start toilet-training earlier with the expectation that young children should be clean and dry by their second birthday. The tendency now is to start toilet-training later, following your baby's lead and starting when he or she seems ready to leave nappies behind and go on to being more grown-up.

However there are often external pressures to start toilet-training. Some parents may want their young child to join a playgroup for a few hours at around two, and this is often the starting age of many playgroups. But whereas playgroups like toilet-trained entrants, this may be too early for your child. Some playgroups are more prepared to help with this, and this may be a better environment for your baby.

There is also the external pressure of a new baby on the way that can motivate parents to start toilet-training. The hope is that it will not be necessary to have to deal with two children in nappies at the same time. But in fact even toilet-trained children can respond to a new baby in the family by doggedly insisting on nappies for themselves again, at least for a while. In the same way, they may insist on being fed by you when the new baby comes, even though they could have been eating more independently for some time. The one-year-old logic behind such U-turns seems to be that this, of all times, does not feel like the right occasion to demonstrate more independence. Young children may need a lot of reassurance that their mother is still there for them, looking after their own baby needs, when the new baby arrives.

Being ready for toilet-training is, once again, linked to feelings of trust. This is not something that can establish itself overnight. It needs nurturing over time. There are also practical reasons for trying to follow your young child's lead with when to start toilet-training. The general feeling among parents is that if they start too early, the whole process simply takes a whole lot longer. If your young child is ready to start, you can work together with the same objective in mind.

Keelan's mother talked about her experience of potty-training her three boys. She said with her first child it seemed to take forever. At one point she felt completely despairing and imagined him as an adolescent in nappies. With her second child she started the whole process later and everything moved along more quickly. When it came to Keelan, she hardly noticed it happening at all and really felt he potty-trained himself. He seemed to make a decision, take off his nappy and, more or less, that was it.

How do young children come to feel ready in this way? Of course they need to be physically ready to contain their bladder and bowel by the development of sphincter control. But they also need to be emotionally ready and this is more complicated.

It may help to start by trying to understand what nappies mean to babies. Their nappies have been a security for them, containing the mess to give to their parent to deal with. Nappies also symbolically represent how they need you to contain and deal with their messy feelings. When they let go of their nappy they are having to let go of it as a trusted physical security but hold on to what it symbolizes in their mind. They have to trust in themselves to find another place to let go of the toilet mess and also trust that their messy feelings can still be contained securely by you in your mind. It is a letting go of one kind of security to be replaced by another. But if babies do not, as yet, have enough trust and dependence in their internal idea of a sufficient container, they are losing one security before they have enough to replace it with.

Building up trust and a sense of security takes time. Just as young children will find their own moment to give up their nappies, they will also sometimes be possessive about the contents of their nappies, not wanting to be changed or cleaned up straight away. As they are working towards becoming more independent, they may feel they would like to be more in charge of this area too. It is a delicate issue and may need to be approached with sensitivity, especially as their wish for more independence and control is what will eventually motivate them towards giving up nappies altogether. For the present, compromises may need to be struck in order to allow your baby as much dignity as possible.

Your one-year-old may not feel ready for potty-training as he or she approaches their second birthday. But the classic signs of telling you when their nappy is full, going to a private place to fill it, getting interested in the toilet or potty (that just happens to be around) or clearly getting impatient with nappies, may all be indications that it's time to begin to think about toilet-training. There are also some excellent children's books that introduce the whole subject in an imaginative and entertaining way. If you have reached the stage when you do not feel pressurized over the whole issue, and feel able to trust yourself to know that your baby does seem ready, this is probably the best time to start.

5

A Life of my Own

The front door and beyond

Looking after your one-year-old at home can be exhausting. When your day has started before 6 a.m., and you can see it stretched out before you in its entirety, having somewhere definite to go at some point during the next twelve hours can feel surprisingly refreshing. Adult company can be a welcome relief and, whether you are a parent or a carer, just getting out of the house can make a huge difference to how you feel about your day. Your baby may well feel the same and an outing is always an adventure.

There are many things you can do outside the home with your one-year-old. One mother of two was looking for a mother's help. A young woman called Ulla, who had been recommended by a friend, arrived to meet her and the children. It had been raining all morning and the mother asked Ulla what she might do with the children on a day like today if she got the job. Ulla replied that she would get their coats and wellies on and take them out looking for puddles to jump in. The older child overheard this and, needless to say, Ulla started that afternoon and the children enjoyed the rain.

Making links with other people in the local area with the same age children is good for the children and adults alike. The park is a favourite place, especially if it has a children's playground. Some parks have a café where adults can meet. Other parks run a One O'clock Club with various art-and-craft activities for young children.

Toy libraries are a popular venue for toddlers and can often provide a calm and stimulating environment where your one-year-old can play to his or her heart's content and sometimes meet up with other children in the neighbourhood. Local drop-in playgroups are also an ideal place to meet up with others and usually provide toys and unstructured activities for the children as well as somewhere for adults to sit and have a coffee. This may be especially helpful if you have a new baby and need to keep your one-year-old entertained while you breast or bottle feed. When your child is more familiar with the new place he or she is more likely to become adventurous and leave your side. Seeing your one-year-old explore this kind of environment is fascinating and you can even enjoy the relative ease of being an observer for some short periods.

Children of this age do not so much play together as play alongside each other. Their interest in other people the same size as themselves is wonderful to watch. Before they start playing they will usually stare at each other a lot and there will possibly be some tentative reaching out and touching. Once past this kind of ritual, they will then tend to get interested in the toys. They may move around the play area, picking up the toys they need, sometimes even handing things to another child, as they become engaged in their own game. All will go well until the unthinkable happens and some other small person tries to take away *what they were playing with*. At this point an adult's coffee break is over.

Learning to share

Sharing does not come naturally to your one-year-old. It is learned behaviour necessary to being part of a civilized social group where everyone's needs are recognized as equally important. For most self-respecting one-year-olds this is a totally alien concept. And it can be a hard lesson to learn.

Josie was clearly pleased when her mother announced a little friend was coming to the house to play with her. The "friend" duly arrived and the children began to play with some toys on the sitting room floor, next to their mothers. But very soon it became obvious that all the toys had found their way to an area just behind Josie, and she seemed to have taken up the position of guarding them. The friend was left with nothing at all to play with. Josie's mother collected more toys from upstairs – taking care to select ones she knew Josie was not especially fond of – but Josie screamed as they were given to the small visitor, much to her mother's embarrassment. The next time this friend came to play, a few weeks later, Josie's mother noticed she had brought her own bag of toys.

We have already talked about playing as an exploration of the world and how a baby's world begins with his or her mother. The baby's interest in everything outside the mother stems from the capacity to be interested in her;

then this interest can be taken further. Following this idea, it may be that Josie's difficulty with sharing had more to do with what her toys symbolized to her rather than the toys themselves. What is so hard for your one-year-old to share is not the toy itself but the idea of sharing a beloved mother with anyone else – this is what the fought-over toy represents. The possessive wish – "I want all of you" – is essentially about a baby's relationship to his or her mother. Linked to this, parents will often notice that if there is a new baby on the way or recently arrived, then sharing toys and possessions can become especially hard.

The way forward is perseverance. Helping young children to share will not only make them more popular with their friends, but also be a reassurance to them. If they always succeed in grabbing everything for themselves and not sharing, they will end up feeling overwhelmed by guilty, destructive feelings. Setting clear boundaries about acceptable behaviour with other children will help your baby feel that his or her own greed and possessiveness is under control and is being contained by you.

If there is a new baby around, or due to be soon, your one-year-old may also need to be reassured by you that there is enough of Mummy to go round and no one is going to be deprived of her. Coming to terms with this idea and having a sibling can help in the process of learning to share, especially when your young child recognizes you are well able to keep all the children in mind.

How to be with a friend

Introducing your baby to other children is fun for your baby and also helps him or her to learn how to be with a friend. Be prepared to be on hand to help. It is not just helping them to share the toys but also helping them to behave in a way that is acceptable. One-year-olds will probably always want to have their own way but they will soon learn that bossing everyone around does not endear them to people. Neither does hitting or other kinds of physical aggression. There are basic rules to civilized behaviour and you will help your child to make friends if you teach him or her the guidelines.

In playgroups there is generally a certain amount of activity across the room with mothers taking their children over to other children to say sorry – this is part of learning. The children not being ferried around in this way tend to be the ones who are hurting others the most. This can make them unpopular and therefore at a disadvantage. In these kinds of social environments, it never helps to turn a blind eye to antisocial behaviour. In fact it is a missed opportunity for helping your child to learn how to be with a friend. If there is a new brother or sister in the family, this is another excellent ongoing opportunity for your one-year-old to learn how to be with other children in a friendly way.

Georgina had a new baby sister, Amy. Georgina's mother talked about how her one-year-old was attacking the new baby and how much this was upsetting her. She didn't know what to do about it. It sometimes happened that the attacks would go unnoticed until too late. What started as Georgina's gentle patting of Amy would gradually develop into slaps. A mouth resting on her head for some time would become a bite that made Amy cry out in pain.

When these kinds of attacks are not seen in time, it leaves the aggression behind them uncontained and even more frightening. Georgina needed to be prevented from hurting Amy in order to feel safe from her own aggression. The continuation of the attacks upset Georgina's mother more and so distanced her further from Georgina. This served only to perpetuate Georgina's hostility towards Amy. The feeling of only sporadic safety from aggressive feelings consequently threatened them all. The family responded to the situation by talking to Georgina about how she sometimes liked the new baby and sometimes didn't like the new baby. Her mother also made a particular effort to have some times alone with her, giving her special attention.

Everyone in the family has a right to protection. A new baby is particularly vulnerable and, as with Georgina, it may be too much to expect your one-year-old to be alone in a room with a new sibling and be able to control upsurges of jealousy. Your one-year-old needs to be protected from his or her own aggressive feelings just as much as the new baby needs protection from attacks.

Working though feelings of jealousy and competition in the family has already been discussed in the context of thinking about your baby's place in the family. A new sibling can stir up so many strong feelings that your one-year-old will need your help to deal with them. A good start is to be clear about the difference between feeling something and doing something. It is OK to feel cross, but not OK to bite. It is OK to feel jealous but not OK to hit. The guidelines of acceptable behaviour can be set within the family and these can then be transferred to your child's contact with other children outside the family. It is all good practice for times ahead.

Your child in a more structured play setting

There are other more structured activities you can introduce your one-year-old to. These include things like music and movement groups, messy art groups, story time groups, physical activity groups and so on. These kinds of groups are teacher led and often require your one-year-old to sit with you as part of a group with a task at hand. This is an achievement in itself for such a young child. The teacher will then lead the group and give instructions. With a varied collection of other one-year-olds in the group, the experience can be quite entertaining. It is also an opportunity for understanding more about your child in a different setting, and you may find you notice things that would not necessarily be so obvious at home.

One of Helen's favourite places to go was the library. Her mother took her every Monday afternoon when it was special story time. The librarian would gather very young children into a group in front of her and then read from a large book, showing the children the pictures as she went along. After a few stories had been read, the children were given crayons and paper to draw a picture about whatever they wanted.

Helen's mother had been concerned that her 22-month-old daughter shrank away from other children when she came across them in the park's Wendy house or at other people's houses. But in the quiet and structured setting of the library story time something else was beginning to happen. Helen started to approach other children in a way her mother had never seen before. She would look at their pictures and show them what she had drawn.

Watching her, Helen's mother realized that her daughter preferred quiet, calm activities. She wondered about Helen's usual apprehensiveness around other children. What had she been nervous about? Had something about the children made her feel unsafe? How could she help her with this? At least one of her questions seemed to be answering itself as she noticed Helen finding her voice and growing in confidence in this calm environment.

Lois's mother took her daughter to Action Kids every week. It was a very lively group with an energetic, enthusiastic teacher called Janice. The children (sometimes holding the hand of their parent or carer) would follow Janice around the room, popping bubbles as fast as she could produce them from her giant bubble blower. Then there would be obstacle courses to negotiate, clothes to dress up in, hats to put on, a giant tent to hide beneath and many other games to play. Lois, just 23 months, joined in with everything, clearly enjoying herself, but her mother noticed she was always a bit tentative with one particular game.

Janice would produce a huge bag of coloured balls and empty them out all over the floor. She would then hold up a ball of a particular colour and ask the children to collect all the ones that were the same and put them in a basket. The children would rush around collecting the balls, running to put them in the right place. Lois, however, looked as though she found this overwhelming. Her mother thought that Lois understood what she needed to do. She would notice a ball but make her way towards it almost deliberately slowly so that it always got grabbed by another child first. Rather than getting upset about this, Lois then seemed to become transfixed by watching what the other children were doing as if this was a much more interesting activity than the ball game. Struggling with the temptation to rugby-tackle other one-year-olds and secure a ball for Lois to get her back in the game, her mother began to recognize something about her daughter and her own unique personality.

What was it about the ball game? Lois's mother didn't have any clear answers, but she had lots of questions. What was it that Lois found overwhelming? Was it the pace of this game, with the colourful balls spilling everywhere and then the rush to find one? Was it the instruction to choose the right colour ball that was too much to take in? Was it a fear of the possibility of conflict with another child who might want the same ball? Or could it be an underlying fear of her own potential competitive aggression that held her back from trying to get the ball, and instead made her focus on exploring this kind of competitiveness in the other children as they played the game?

Daniel's mother had a different situation. She decided to take 20-month-old Daniel to a local music group led by a smiling, animated musician called Sudah. Unfortunately the group started during Daniel's afternoon nap time so he had fallen asleep in his buggy on the way and slept through the whole hour. His mother stayed, wondering if he might wake up, and took the opportunity to watch how the group was run. There was lots of singing, clapping, actions and playing musical instruments. But the highlight of the group was when Sudah brought out a large hand-held drum with a rather mesmerizing colourful swirl decorating the drumskin. There was a hush. Sudah invited the children to come up one at a time and bang the drum with her stick. A few children dared to approach the drum with awed ceremony. One parent commented to Daniel's mother that her little boy had been coming to this music group for months and had only just had his first try. The following week Daniel skipped his nap and banged the drum, rather hard, so that even Sudah seemed surprised.

Although Daniel's mother was pleased he banged the drum, it made her wonder about his forcefulness. Something about it made her recount a habit of his that started at some stage during his breastfeeding days when he would take his mother's little finger in his hand and hold it very tenderly as he fed. This habit had continued and now, at 22 months, it was still manifesting itself but with variations. When he was close to his mother he would take her "ickle fingie" in his hand and begin to stroke and squeeze it gently. This continued for a while until finally a not-quite-so-gentle squeeze obliged her to take her hand away.

Daniel's mother also had lots of questions. For a start, she wondered why he did it. What is it that turns a gentle caress into something hard and painful? Was it linked to the forceful way he beat the drum? Was it a positive thing? Could he be showing how he is capable of having ambivalent feelings — loving on the one hand and hostile on the other? Is this what he felt towards her? Was it something about the dependency of such loving feelings that felt painful? Was this why the caress was withdrawn and turned into something more unfriendly?

Being curious about your child and asking yourself endless questions are all ways towards understanding his or her personality. Noticing what suits them, following their lead, developing a picture of them in your mind and building on that picture each day — this all helps them to be known by you. Seeing young children in a rather more structured setting can often help you see what they are able to cope with and what they find more difficult. It can also be heartening for parents to notice the kinds of circumstances in which their baby blossoms. As well as helping you to understand your child, the experience of being in more structured settings — with you to help — will allow your one-year-old to become gently accustomed to the kind of environment that he or she will eventually need to manage in without you.

Conclusion: Looking forward with hope

We started by thinking about how it might be possible to imagine yourself into the mind of a one-year-old. Capturing the essence of his or her experience – trying to understand your child – not only fulfils your wish as a parent, but also fulfils your child's emotional need to be understood and have his or her feelings contained by you. It is a profoundly creative, empathetic process and endlessly challenging. Sometimes the demands of the task can feel overwhelming and being emotionally supported yourself makes a tremendous difference. Of course, the value of what you are doing cannot be overestimated. Parents' understanding allows children to be known as they really are and helps them to feel grounded in their own personality.

The process of understanding and the channels of communication between parent and child are there from the beginning. They do not rely on words – English, Spanish or otherwise – but are more to do with a state of mind that is open to the baby. Holding and containing your baby's experience in your mind involves a loving thoughtfulness. In this context, your baby's world of language and imagination develops hand in hand. Stories – your baby's own and those of others – become an enriching part of life. At around the same time, he or she may be taking first steps both physically and emotionally, and confidence is building.

The value of your baby's exploration and curiosity has far-reaching implications. It starts with the exploration of his or her mother and then extends into the wider world. Playtime, with all its joy and fun, broadens the scope even further as feelings and anxieties are explored and contained through the arena of play. Babies' interest in containers – something you will see over and over again in their play – reflects their need for emotional containment as they dare to focus further afield. Imaginative games open up the world even further and help your child explore his or her own internal landscape. At the same time they can lead your child to explore safely whatever is being experienced in external reality.

Different families in various different situations provide other rich grounds for discovery as your baby's relationships with family members become increasingly important. Your baby will also be exploring ideas in his or her mind and the helpful idea of a united couple may be beginning to take root in the midst of Oedipal phantasies about parents. As family life goes on, with family meals as frequent reference points, your baby will continue explorations in the arena of new tastes and textures in food. Struggles with feelings of littleness and dependency may link closely to the historically dependent feeding relationship between mother and baby. Young children may need to make some empowering choices of their own – possibly about breakfast cereal – to counterbalance this position.

As such choices are made and your one-year-old becomes more assertive, his or her personality starts to crystallize. Developing a sense of individual identity becomes a priority. Whether your one-year-old is your firstborn or one in a larger family, his or her place in the family has particular consequences, and this place may be subject to change. A newborn baby in the family is a huge event and one that your young child is deeply affected by. Young children will have their own opinions about this – about where the new baby sleeps, for instance – as they have in other matters. Respecting your child's opinion and allowing for different opinions in the family also means holding your own. Sometimes it is in your baby's best interests to hear a final "No". But he or she may get into a temper about it. Clear boundaries and sensitive handling will help with your young child's temper tantrum. Your understanding and containment will also ease the fears that such hot tantrum-like feelings can transform into. Angry, frustrated feelings that are projected out into the world can come back with a vengeance to haunt your one-year-old. He or she will need to have those fears and phobias contained and recognized for what they are from a more balanced adult perspective. In this way they will diminish and gradually fade into the background.

Your baby's greatest fear, however, is being without you. Recognizing the value of brief separations does not mean any lack of appreciation of your baby's pain at being away from you. The pain is there because of his or her depth of love. It is the pain of intimacy and it is denied and rejected at great emotional cost. When your eyes are open to seeing it and containing the pain on your child's behalf, he or she is more able to express it and so stay in touch with these feelings. Your baby's capacity to hold a helpful, containing idea of you in the mind sees him or her through many different kinds of goodbyes. The development of this idea depends on trust and all you can do to build this trust is helpful. The achievements of sleeping and toilet-training are also linked to your baby's growing trust. Everything takes time.

Finally we thought about your baby's world outside the front door and the benefits of become involved in different social groups. Learning to share and how to be with a friend are ways to help your one-year-old as he or she steps out into the beginnings of a more independent life. These are brave steps and each one is taken at some emotional cost – there is always the issue of what may be left behind. But moving forward is hugely optimistic and full of adventure. Seeing young children in more structured play settings can offer extra opportunities to understand and help them with each further step they are brave enough to take.

We have ended with many questions from different parents about their children because this is the reality. Every parent is in this position when it comes to their child and there are seldom enough answers to meet the demand. As much as parents will try to understand their one-year-old, the task will never be complete. Like adults, children have minds that no one can ever fully know. But asking the questions and being curious is the only way forward. If you can do this in relation to your child, recognizing that you may not always have the answer but still being interested enough to ask the question, you will also be instilling in them the compelling idea of interest and curiosity as a way of life. Your child is at the beginning of life in the wider world. It is full of unknowns for him or her. If you can tolerate not knowing and survive, then your young child will also be helped to tolerate something of the same experience. It does not stop you searching.

There will be times ahead when you will not be with your baby. As he or she grows older, spending more hours away from you will be a natural and positive move forward. What parents want for their children is that they can take this step with confidence, looking forward with hope. Such a state of mind is what you have been working towards from the very beginning. This kind of independence is not the same as your child leaving you and doing it on his or her own. Rather it involves trusting and depending on helpful parental figures – a united couple – as such figures gradually become established at the root of your child's personality. These helpful, reliable figures can eventually become his or her own inner resources, there to guide and encourage your child through life.

At such a young age, your one-year-old is continuing to build up inner resources of this kind. He or she will rely on you for repeated reassurances and confirmations that build up confidence in such a helpful internal idea. If this good idea can take root it will always be there to emotionally nourish your child in the years ahead, encouraging him or her towards a life of full potential. It is essentially an idea full of optimism and hope in the future.

Further Reading

For your one-year-old baby

Ahlberg, A. and Howard, P. (1998) *Mocking Bird*. London: Walker.

Anonymous (1997) *What's That? A First Word and Picture Book*. London: Campbell.

Ayto, R. and Cottringer, A. (1997) *Ella and the Naughty Lion*. London: Mammoth.

Bradman, T. and Amstutz, A. (1996) *Just Us Three*. London: HarperCollins.

Burningham, J. (1994) *Avocado Baby*. London: Red Fox.

Cornell, L.J. and Cony, F. (1998) *The Timid Tortoise*. London: Tango.

Hawkins, C. and Hawkins, J. (1993) *Where's My Mummy?* London: Walker.

Seuss, Dr (1980) *Green Eggs and Ham*. London: Collins.

Thompson, C. (1991) *Baby Days*. London: Orchard.

Waddell, M. and Dale, P. (1992) *Rosie's Babies*. London: Walker.

Ziefert, H. and Boon, E. (1988) *Mummy, Where Are You?* London: Puffin.

About your one-year-old baby

Daws, D. (1989) *Through the Night: Helping Parents and Sleepless Infants*. London: Free Association.

Fraiberg, S. (1968) *The Magic Years: Understanding and Handling the Problems of Early Childhood*. London: Methuen.

Harris, M. (1983) *Thinking about Infants and Young Children*. Strath Tay: Clunie Press.

Helpful organizations

Association for Post-Natal Illness
145 Dawes Road
Fulham
London SW6 7EB
Tel: 020 7386 0868
www.apni.org
Support for women with post-natal depression

Cry-sis
BM Cry-sis
London WC1N 3XX
Tel: 020 7404 5011 (seven days a week, 9 a.m. to 10 p.m.)
www.cry-sis.com
Helpline for families with excessively crying or sleepless babies

Exploring Parenthood
Latimer Education Centre
194 Freston Road
London W10 6TT
Tel: 020 88964 1827
Parents' Advice Line: 020 8960 1678

Gingerbread Association for One Parent Families
7 Sovereign Close
Sovereign Court
London E1W 2HW
Tel: 020 7488 9300
Advice line: 0800 018 4318
www.gingerbread.org.uk
Support for single parent families

Home-Start
2 Salisbury Road
Leicester LE1 7QR
Tel: 0116 233 9955
www.home-start.org.uk
Practical and emotional support for parents in their own home.

Local SureStart Organisation (in the UK)
SureStart Unit
DfES and DWP
Level 2, Caxton House
Tothill Street
London SW1H 9NA
Tel: 0870 000 2288
www.surestart.gov.uk

National Childbirth Trust
Alexandra House, Oldham Terrace
Acton
London W3 6NH
Tel: 0870 444 8707
www.nctpregnancyandbabycare.com
Information and support for parents

Parentline Plus
Tel: 0808 800 2222 (helpline 24 hours a day)
www.parentlineplus.org.uk
Information and support for parents

Parents Anonymous
Tel: 020 7233 9955 (7 p.m. to midnight)
www.parentsanonymous.org
Helpline for parents

PlayMatters/National Association of Toy and Leisure Libraries
68 Churchway
London NW1 1LT
Tel: 020 7255 4600
www.playmatters.co.uk

Pre-school Learning Alliance
61–63 Kings Cross Road
London WC1X 9LL
Tel: 020 7833 0991
www.pre-school.org.uk

Under-fives Counselling Service
The Tavistock Clinic
120 Belsize Lane
London NW3 5BA
Tel: 020 7435 7111
www.tavi-port.org (under Patient Services, Infant Mental Health Service)

YoungMinds/National Association for Child and Family Mental Health
102–108 Clerkenwell Road
London EC1M 5SA
Tel: 020 7336 8445
Parents' Information Service: 0800 018 2138
www.youngminds.org.uk

Index